ZAKIR HUSSAIN

ZAKIR HUSSAIN

A Life in Music

In Conversation with Nasreen Munni Kabir

HarperCollins *Publishers* India

First published in hardback in India by HarperCollins *Publishers* 2018

This edition published in India by HarperCollins *Publishers* 2024
4th Floor, Tower A, Building No 10, DLF Cyber City,
DLF Phase II, Gurugram – 122002
www.harpercollins.co.in

2 4 6 8 10 9 7 5 3 1

Text Copyright © Zakir Hussain and Nasreen Munni Kabir 2018, 2024

P-ISBN: 978-93-6213-387-8
E-ISBN: 978-93-5277-050-2

The views and opinions expressed in this book are the authors' own
and the facts are as reported by them, and the publishers are not in
any way liable for the same.

Zakir Hussain and Nasreen Munni Kabir assert the moral right
to be identified as the authors of this work.

All photographs are from the Zakir Hussain Collection unless the photographer's
name is expressly mentioned, in which case the copyright is theirs. In the event
that the name of an individual photographer has been inadvertently uncredited,
HarperCollins would be happy to include this information on notification by
the concerned individual in subsequent editions, if any.

All rights reserved. No part of this publication may be reproduced,
stored in a retrieval system, or transmitted, in any form or by any means,
electronic, mechanical, photocopying, recording or otherwise,
without the prior permission of the publishers.

Typeset in 12.5/16.5 Arno Pro at SŪRYA, New Delhi

Printed and bound at
Manipal Technologies Limited, Manipal

This book is produced from independently certified FSC® paper to ensure
responsible forest management.

Introduction

In the mid-1980s, I happened to spot Zakir Hussain in a well-known store in Bombay's Taj Mahal Hotel. I had not met him formally before that day, but he appeared to be an approachable kind of person, despite being a world-famous musician. However, greeting him without any introduction seemed an invasion of his privacy. And, after all, what could I say? That he played the tabla brilliantly, his dexterity and skill were magical to watch on stage, that I loved his music? Instead, I discreetly followed his movements around the shop from the corner of my eye, but just as he was about to leave the store, he gave me a lovely smile and said hello. Even though some forty years have passed since that random encounter, I can still recall his warmth and friendliness.

Since that time, and in many cities of the world, I have seen Zakir Hussain perform with a variety of musicians, both Indian and international. His extraordinary playing and the extreme sense of rigour that he brings to his art are clearly manifest.

Among the many cherished evenings with Zakir's music, a most memorable one was seeing the path-breaking Shakti on stage in the 1970s. The Shakti sound was so exhilarating that I felt I was on an airport runway and my heart was about to take off.

The training that Zakir Hussain received under his father, the extraordinary Allarakha, started at a very young age, but it was not long before he began to receive acclaim for his own sound and style. As a musician, Zakir Hussain was considered a child prodigy; today he is considered a genius. Despite the international reputation and huge following that he now has, he wears his fame lightly. He remains a man of tehzeeb and humility. Zakir has broken many records and won many awards, but is always the first to credit the 'Holy Trinity' of tabla players, Pandit Samta Prasad, Pandit Kishan Maharaj and his father, for their groundbreaking contribution to music, and for the fact that they elevated the very status of the tabla in the first place.

Having worked on a number of conversation-based books with the leading names of Indian cinema, I felt bold enough to try and approach this gifted musician with the idea of doing a similar book. Although I am neither a musicologist nor a music expert, I believe the discipline and passion that drive many artists to keep growing, whether as film-makers or musicians, are much the same. And so I convinced myself that even if my questions were not those of an expert, Zakir Hussain's answers would help music lovers like myself to better understand his music and to discover the path his life has taken. There is so much to learn from Zakir Hussain.

He is a musician who has for over six decades practised the art of the tabla, playing not only with four generations of master musicians of India, but accompanying many greats from the worlds of Western classical, rock and jazz.

I finally plucked up the courage to ask my friends Ayesha Sayani (affectionately known as Pooh) and Sumantra Ghosal if they could introduce us. I had seen Sumantra's wonderful documentary, *The Speaking Hand: Zakir Hussain and the Art of the Indian Drum*, and knew that if they believed I could do justice to the subject, they would encourage me, and if not, I would be dissuaded. Ayesha, who had read some of my books, was instantly enthusiastic and said the best way forward was that she first introduce me by email, and that I then send a formal letter outlining the idea for a book and requesting to meet him on his next visit to Bombay.

It was entirely through the generosity of Ayesha Sayani and Sumantra Ghosal that, in January 2016, the four of us met. Since the meeting took place after the lunch hour at a well-known Bombay restaurant, we had the restaurant to ourselves. Zakir patiently heard me out as I explained that my area of research was cinema and not music, to which he said, 'So this would be a leap of faith? In any case, I do not want a how-to-play-the-tabla book.' Our meeting ended with him saying that he'd get back to me once he had read some of my books.

A few weeks later, Zakir phoned and very matter-of-factly gave me the go-ahead. I was absolutely delighted and immediately called Ayesha Sayani to share the news. I will always be grateful to Ayesha and Sumantra for encouraging me throughout, and believing that the book would happen. I extend my thanks to them again here.

For the following two years, between 2016 and August 2017, Zakir Hussain and I met in various cities—Bombay, Pune, London and even Antwerp. Each of our fifteen sessions lasted for about two hours. Our conversations, mostly in English, peppered with Hindi/Urdu, were recorded on a small digital recorder and then transcribed. As many of the events we talked about date to the period prior to the renaming of Bombay to Mumbai, Calcutta to Kolkata and Madras to Chennai, I have used the original city names for consistency.

Working around the clock, Zakir also travels to every corner of the globe and gives about 200 concerts a year, but despite the pressure on his time, when he answered my questions he gave full and thoughtful attention. In London, we met at whichever hotel he happened to be staying at, and in Bombay, we talked in his home in Simla House—a place that has been witness to over fifty years of Qureshi family history. In the course of our many conversations, his vast knowledge of every kind of music was evident, and his understanding of form and tradition, multilayered and insightful.

Zakir has a very quick and analytic mind. With his intuitive and instant reading of the musical expression of the artist with whom he is playing, it is no wonder that he can so easily accompany many different kinds of musicians. His years of teaching tabla in America and interacting with music students from all over the world is perhaps why he is also able to explain difficult musical concepts in a clear and accessible way. In fact, he can converse on any subject and has a natural flow of ideas with a phenomenal memory for anecdotes and incidents—many fascinating stories are recorded here as he remembers his encounters with the great names in music.

Zakir Hussain is noticeably personable and friendly, but is also someone who likes doing things in a certain order—so if I happened to rush him, he would stop me and slow the pace down. The perfectionist in him would also lose patience with any errors that he would spot in our working drafts. It was important to him that things were 'just so'.

This book has taken over two years to complete, and I hope it will serve as an introduction to an intelligent and thoughtful man who happens to be a truly exceptional musician. I believe only a multi-volume biography can even start to cover the many aspects of his life's work and I hope this book is a step towards this possibility. Here, I will add it is with the meticulous eye of his wife, Antonia Minnecola, that errors were avoided, facts were checked and words flowed smoothly. She is instrumental in the completion of this book, and I will always be grateful to her for her help and encouragement.

Getting to know Zakir Hussain through the process of writing this book and to learn about music from a musician so gifted and yet who still has a sense of openness to take that leap of faith has been an immense privilege.

NASREEN MUNNI KABIR

Zakir Hussain (ZH): From the very start we were somehow tied together—me and my dad. I was always very attached to him. As a child, I remember I used to stay up late into the night and refuse to sleep until he came home, and only then did I go to bed.

Around the time that I was born, my father was suffering from a heart ailment and was extremely unwell. Someone had told my mother that I was an unlucky child because my birth coincided with this most distressing time for the family. My father, whom we called Abba, was so critically ill at that time that many of his colleagues and friends came to say a last goodbye. This included Raj Kapoor, Nargis and Ashok Kumar, who starred in *Bewafa*, a film for which Abba had composed the music.

My mother did not breastfeed me when I was brought home. She really believed that I was unlucky, and so a close friend of the family who lived near us in the mohalla of the Mahim dargah [neighbourhood of the shrine of the saint Hazrat Makhdoom Ali Shah] looked after me. I sadly don't remember the name of this kind lady, but she became a sort of surrogate mother to me for the first few weeks. You can imagine this was out of the ordinary because the eldest son in an Indian family is usually treated like a prince.

I was told that a holy man called Gyani Baba appeared at our door soon after my birth. He called out to my mother by her name, Bavi Begum. No one had a clue how he happened to know her name, but somehow he did. My mother went out to meet him and Gyani Baba looked at her and said: 'You have a son. The next four years are very dangerous for him, so look after him well. He'll save your husband. Name the child Zakir Hussain.'

Hussain is not the family name. My surname should have been either Qureshi or Allarakha Qureshi. But Gyani Baba insisted that I must be called Zakir Hussain; he also said that I should become a fakir of Hazrat Imam Hussain, the grandson of the Prophet.

One of the duties of a fakir is to go to seven houses during Muharram and ask for alms. The purpose of this is to learn humility. The fakir must then give whatever he has received to those poorer than himself. So, as a toddler, during Muharram, my mother would dress me in a green kurta, give me a jhola to carry and we'd go from house to house in our neighbourhood asking for alms. People gave me a little money or some sweets. Whatever I was given went straight to the mosque or to the Mahim shrine. When I was older, I continued this practice during all the years that I lived in India. Even when we moved to Nepean Sea Road in the 1960s, I would go back to Mahim during Muharram, and when I moved away to America, for many years, Amma continued this penance in my place.

Another thing that Gyani Baba told Amma was to watch over me, and, sure enough, for the first four years of my life,

I kept falling sick. I would accidentally drink kerosene, or my body would be covered with unexplained boils, or I would suddenly get a high fever; maybe it was typhoid or something. But the interesting thing was, the worse that I got, the better my father became. As Gyani Baba had predicted, four years later Abba was fit and well, and by that time, I was in good health too.

So that's how I got my name.

Nasreen Munni Kabir (NMK): And 'Zakir' means? The one who remembers?

ZH: It can mean the one who remembers, or the one who does zikr, which is a form of devotion that involves rhythmically repeating Allah's name, or repeating a mantra-like chant. Zikr is part of the Sufi tradition, and the whirling dervishes, for example, also practise zikr to attain God. So Zakir is the one who does zikr—my name means something like that.

NMK: I did not know the story behind your naming. What an intriguing start to a hugely eventful life. I am just wondering if Gyani Baba was a Muslim or a Hindu.

ZH: He was not a Muslim. In later years, I asked my elder sister Khurshid Apa about him and she said all she knew was that he cooked his own food and carried it around with him because he did not want to eat food made by another hand.

In those days, it did not matter if Gyani Baba was a Muslim or a Hindu. I guess even being Sunni or Shia did not really matter—perhaps for the hierarchy it did matter—but for most people it didn't. Many musicians followed Shia Islam and in those days, many worked among baijis in kothas, so they would not perform during Muharram.

One Muharram, I remember going to a majlis [a gathering to remember Hazrat Imam Hussain] with my father to Bade Ghulam Ali Khansahib's house. There were many musicians there—it was something like the salons in old Europe where a candle was passed to each artist who then recited a poem or sang—here a paan-daan (usually an ornamental silver paan box) was passed around. Whether the paan-daan was passed to an instrumentalist or a vocalist, once it was placed in front of the musician, he would sing a 'naat'. These devotional songs only had a few verses, and since the singers would melodically embellish the naats of their choice, each performance would last about twenty minutes and then the paan-daan would move on to the next person and the next. It was very interesting to watch.

NMK: Do you think a recording of those evenings exists? The singing must have been beautiful.

ZH: I don't know. Most musicians did not own a tape recorder in those days. In fact, we didn't either, not until the mid-1960s when my father brought a Philips tape recorder from America. In any case, I doubt if they would have let the majlis be recorded because it was not a performance. They sang for God.

As for me, I could not sing a whole naat, but I could say a few lines. I was just a little kid, a spectator, who was sitting around. Abba would sing and later he composed some naats in films that had a Muslim setting.

NMK: What is your first memory? I mean from your childhood.

ZH: A first memory as a child? There are quite a few things I remember. It's hard to think of the very first memory. [*long pause*] Our first home in Mahim was a little room. I was about two or three years old. I remember our tiny kitchen very clearly. It wasn't a kitchen-kitchen. You walked through the door into the room and you could see a small cemented square area that had a drain—there was a four-foot wall cordoning it off, and on the other side of the wall, a kerosene stove was placed on the floor. Amma had lined up pots and pans against the wall and she would sit on what was called a 'patara'—a very low wooden stool with short legs—while she cut vegetables. To get the kerosene stove going, Amma would have to use an air pump and then she'd cook on that stove. I remember taking a cooking pot from that tiny kitchen, turning it over and drumming on it. Yeah!

Another memory that comes to mind was when I was about three and I saw Abba riding back and forth on the street on a bicycle. I thought that was cute! Here's this ustad on a bicycle, weaving his way up and down the neighbourhood. The cycle must have belonged to some student of his who happened to be visiting, and my father had probably decided on a whim to try riding it. Abba had a big grin on his face and everyone around him had even bigger grins on their faces. That's a happy memory. [*smiles*]

NMK: Did your father lose his temper easily?

ZH: No, no. He was not an angry man. He was very calm. I never saw him get upset with his students either. If they messed up, he would say, '*Dhat teri ki, kya hai?*' [Damn it! What's wrong?]

There was no screaming and shouting, none of that. He never hit me, except for once. I think I was about nine. He slapped me because I had broken my third finger while playing cricket. And that was a no-no as far as he was concerned. I was going to use those hands to play the tabla. When he slapped me, I had tears in my eyes and he didn't like that, and so he gave me a hug and took me to the Sindhi chaat shop nearby and got me a plate of dahi batata puri. [*smiles*]

NMK: We were to start our conversations yesterday (20 May 2015), but we missed our first appointment. I knocked on your hotel door, but you didn't hear me. You had just landed in London and when we spoke later, you said you had fallen asleep with your earphones on. What were you listening to?

ZH: Tomorrow I'm playing at the Royal Festival Hall with three Indian musicians and a group of Celtic musicians—some are from Scotland and others from Ireland and Brittany in France. I was listening to their music, so when I meet them today for rehearsals, I can say: 'You remember that song you played? Well, the Indians have come up with this idea to go with that, shall we try it?' That's better than asking what we should play and then looking at each other in the hope that someone might suggest something.

When I play with different musicians, and sometimes it could be for the first time, it is important to know how they express themselves musically. To know what appeals to them in terms of tonality, or what kind of pitches they favour, so that I can bring a set of instruments to support those pitches and tones.

Say, if I'm going to play with a jazz band, I listen to their albums, read their interviews and familiarize myself with their music. It's a way of showing respect and that I am not just arriving at the concert hall thinking: 'Oh, I'm going to play with you, we'll see what that's like in the dressing room.'

NMK: So you immerse yourself in their world of music. Have you always prepared to play with your fellow musicians in this way?

ZH: I am not playing an entirely fixed piece of music, but music that requires some spontaneity. Creating something new does not always happen on the spot, therefore understanding a musical style allows me to rearrange things a little, to mix and match. It's like seeing a flower in a vase, and it looks good, but you know if you turned the flower, it could look just that bit different.

Being aware of musical styles is definitely prevalent in the jazz world in the West, the white world or the black world, or whatever you want to call it. You'll find jazz musicians constantly listening to other musicians, especially if they are going to play music together.

NMK: One always thinks of jazz as improvisation, but you're talking about researching. Improvising within a framework.

ZH: It is research because music is a conversation. And a proper conversation can only happen if you know each other well. If you're just strangers, you say: 'Hello, how are you?' 'I'm okay, thank you.' That's fine, but your connection won't go very deep. And yes, it's definitely within a framework. It has to be, otherwise we would be meandering along on the stage with no head or tail, without an idea of how to begin or end.

You're asking me questions, but they're not off the top of your head; you've prepared, you know how you want to begin each session. Our conversation may branch off into a zillion directions and that's great, but there has to be some research and understanding. I think it's a sign of respect for each other to have that.

NMK: Was research needed when you started to play with Indian musicians?

ZH: I was very lucky. From the age of seven, I sat on the stage with Abba whilst he played with so many greats. It was a lived experience for me, and it allowed me to absorb all that I had heard over the years.

When I accompanied Pandit Ravi Shankarji, the great sitarist, all those recordings and concerts were in my head. I could close my eyes and see Raviji and my father looking at each other during a performance, smiling, nodding. I could visualize Abba doing something and Raviji responding with a wonderful emotion, or vice versa.

Those memories allowed me to provide the kind of support that Ravi Shankarji expected of me when we played together. He was the main artist and I was the accompanist. My response to him was based on my familiarity with his music—perhaps it was not the response that my father gave him; it was bound to be slightly different because I have a different temperament—my tone, phraseology and sounds are different. My playing probably had an element of surprise and that may have sparked a different chain of events.

NMK: Does this element of surprise inspire the lead musician?

ZH: Inspiration comes because the lead musician is in his comfort zone. You don't just throw him off a mountain without a parachute. He has to be in his comfort zone, and then he or she will react with a fresh thought. Total surprise can be dangerous, at least in the world of music. I don't put a completely different idea from left-field on the table. I react in the way I'm required to.

Audiences who come to my concerts know that my concerts are not just about me. They are about the music that I represent and the musicians involved in that tradition. Recently, an MC said in more or less these words when she introduced us on the London stage: 'Zakir Hussain is accompanied by the sitar player Niladri Kumar.'

That's wrong. I could not correct her immediately because we were standing in the wings, but when we went on to the stage, I said: 'It's actually the other way round. I'm accompanying Niladri Kumar; that's the traditional role of the tabla—to accompany. In the second half, the orchestra will accompany me and the tabla shall be presented as a solo instrument. Let's see how it works.'

That's the right way of introducing the lead musician, no matter who it is—Niladri Kumar, Rakesh Chaurasia, Sabir Khan, or Dilshad Khan.

NMK: When you go home after a concert, how do you unwind?

ZH: The unwinding has to take place. In the old days, you had a glass of water, took a deep breath, and a few friends would come to the green room and say, '*Kya baat hai!*' [Wow! Excellent!] You felt grateful that it had gone well. You came home and sat down to eat. From this large gathering, there's finally just you, your wife and your kids and you enter a calm environment. How shall I put it? You return to the womb in which you feel this comforting warmth; it just relaxes you.

It's when you're in bed alone that the downturn from the high really begins and you start replaying the concert. I find myself dissecting everything; the good moments, and the not-so-good ones. It is very difficult for me to fall asleep immediately. I have to run the evening over and over in my head because I just need to—there are musicians who can move on instantly, but for me, it's important to absorb what I have just done. After about an hour in bed, I give up trying to sleep, so I read a book or watch TV, and try to slow the mind down.

My father was totally different. He would lie on his side with his head on the pillow and talk, while tapping rhythms on his knee. I'd massage his arms, up and down, and he would quietly fall asleep. But Abba's fingers would still be moving—he was still at the concert and in the moment when something good was happening.

The whole concert is not necessarily the beginning and end of it all. There are only a few moments, which are gold, the real McCoy. When you're alone you try and remember those moments and recall how they came about. Trying to repeat them never works either; they just happened because you did something; the sitar player did something and it all fell into place to become something magnificent.

NMK: It's magical for the audience to witness a moment when a performance rises to another plane. After so many years of interacting with audiences all around the world, can you gauge audience reaction easily?

ZH: I think audiences are much the same everywhere. The world knows about the world today. There is nothing about Rwanda that people in Oregon can't discover. You can learn about everything wherever you are.

Gauging audiences today is more about my ability to plant a new thought in their minds. I have the confidence now to explore musical ideas that are more challenging in some ways—I don't worry so much about what the audience thinks. You'll find young musicians concerned about how the audience reacts. I was like that too when I was twenty or twenty-five—it was a whole different connection. I used to be direct, more eye to eye. In a solo concert, I told stories, created visuals, and did all sorts of stuff, and sometimes I even elaborated on an idea based, on the reaction of the audience. It worked fantastically, but now I don't even announce what I'm going to do. I just start playing.

Here, I'll take Ravi Shankarji's example. From the late 1960s to almost the early 1980s, he conversed a lot with his audience. He talked to them about the music and joked with them. He became a little more closed later in life and I wondered why—it was not that he had run out of things to say—it was just that he probably thought to himself: 'They know enough about me, Ravi Shankar, so I have the confidence that they'll take this journey with me. I can now explore the depths that exist in music, as opposed to worrying: "Are they with me or not?"'

I think you get to a point in your professional life where the connection with the audience comes from their familiarity with what you do.

NMK: Are there some performances that you avoid?

ZH: I don't play at private gatherings, corporate events or weddings. I just don't. Those are places where people come to socialize, to drink and perhaps have a meal. That's not the way music should be heard.

For me, it's the concert hall or the theatre—people take their seats, the hall darkens and we musicians take our place. Now the audience's focus is fully on the stage. I have often said that the first fifteen minutes of a concert are the most important because artists and audience are establishing contact and a zillion other things cannot happen at the same time. I don't allow photographers to walk around when we start playing. I have always requested the organizers to kindly close the doors as soon as the concert begins, and not to let anybody in until there is a little lull and then latecomers can take their seats. They do that in Western classical concerts. It's nothing new.

NMK: Does it matter to you if the audience is made up of four thousand people or forty? Do you prefer a smaller audience?

ZH: A small audience allows for intimacy. Music transmits better; especially traditional music, which requires interaction between audience and artist. If you're within touching distance of each other and you have eye contact, the experience is something very special. When I'm talking with you, there should be that spark of understanding of what is being said.

I look for that acceptance; my ego requires that my playing is getting across.

When you are in a 4,000-seater, you have no clue what's happening back there. The energy, the strength and power that a note has in the first or third row is not the same twenty rows back. You can hear the music, enjoy it, and even feel its depth in a large hall, but a fuller experience only happens in an intimate gathering—the kind that you have in a one-on-one conversation. It's not unlike chamber music concerts in the Western classical tradition and you understand why these are sought after.

When someone like Vilayat Khansahib or Bismillah Khansahib played in a small mehfil, talking and playing invariably came together: '*Arey mian, yeh Dada ustad ki cheez hai, yeh main suna raha hoon, suno. Isme dekho yeh sur kaise lag raha hai.*' [I'll play a master's composition for you. How do these notes sound?]

Intimacy is also important because we musicians can try out new things because we know we're performing for like-minded people, and the reaction of that small gathering might legitimize what we happen to be working on.

NMK: It sounds like the experience of listening to jazz in a club.

ZH: The small baithaks were exactly like that. It did not matter to the musicians that they were not getting much money because the audience was small, but they happily performed for twice as long as they would have perhaps in Birla Hall or Shanmukhananda Hall.

Intimate concerts are definitely something that I personally look forward to. That's why I love playing at Prithvi Theatre. I don't get paid for the memorial concert, nor do I expect to be paid.

NMK: You're no doubt referring to Jennifer Kendal's memorial concert that's held every year on 28 February at Prithvi in Bombay. I had the good fortune of attending those events for two years running. Crowds of people queued up for hours before the start time because they knew they were in for a treat.

Can you tell us something about the early concerts? I mean before you started performing in large city halls and auditoriums.

ZH: We used to play in big pandals. You could hear the sound of the traffic and the trains going by. What I noticed was that the musicians would maintain eye contact with some people in the audience. I did the same thing too and that connection sort of spread to the people around them and behind them. It's a chain reaction, a ripple effect.

I think most musicians would agree that playing music could also be a visual experience. To me the emotional content of music requires visuals. When I'm playing, I see images, paintings, landscapes and animals. I see different human beings. Assimilation, analysis and emulation—all of this has to happen at the same time during a performance.

NMK: I imagine you've played thousands of concerts over the years. I wonder if there's a list somewhere of all your performances.

ZH: I doubt it. I don't even have photographs. In the early days, having a camera was a luxury, and as a tabla player, you know, we did not make much money. Now it's different; we tabla players are not taken for granted.

In the early days when we were going to play outside Bombay, we tabla players were asked to travel by train whilst the main artists would travel by air. That changed in my father's time and now all the musicians travel together.

It took about twenty years to get to a point where I could ask for something, tell the organizers that I needed this or that.

NMK: Ask for something? What do you mean?

ZH: Say, I wanted a good hotel room, or I preferred to travel by air—it took twenty years before I could ask the organizers. It didn't really matter. Things happened in an organic way, but when they did, they stuck.

NMK: Do you remember how old you were when you flew for the first time?

ZH: I think I was about twelve. Abba and I were travelling from Bombay to Indore in a Dakota, those twin-engine planes. I remember going to the toilet and throwing up because I was not used to flying, so my father decided that we should take the train back home. So we took the metre-gauge all the way from Indore to Ratlam and from Ratlam we got the Frontier Mail to Bombay.

NMK: Was it just you and your father? Did you talk a lot on the journey?

ZH: The social skills of Indian classical musicians of the past were limited. They spent 98 per cent of their time with their music. It would have been great if Abba could have discussed politics, science or maths. But no, it was always music. He could talk for hours about rhythms, melodies and the old masters. Even when Abba was asked to speak at a press conference, he would say: 'I'm sorry, I can't speak, only my hands can.' But if he were asked about music, he would perk up and talk with ease.

Performers must have a certain amount of ego—have that confidence to get on to the stage and strut their stuff. In a negative form, the ego creates friction. We are fallible as humans. Our greatness, if we are in any way great, is only as musicians. These are two different things. So that's why some of the old masters, outside of their music, were not necessarily good husbands, good parents or even of great value to the community. This is not meant as a criticism; it's just that their commitment to their art was total.

NMK: Have musicians always been respected by all strata of society?

ZH: We must remember that they were socially unacceptable in the India of the 1950s and '60s. They were seen as lower-class citizens and did not really socialize with the elite. Of course, musicians were respected and were asked to perform and so on, but they were very rarely invited into the homes of the higher echelons.

Perhaps it was because musicians chose to talk only about music. Musicians of that era were very intelligent, smart and had a sixth sense—how else could they have transmitted their art form to others? So I think it was a personal choice to shun the idea of interacting with people on other levels. My father, Ali Akbar Khansahib, Bade Ghulam Ali Khansahib or Amir Khansahib—they were all like that. It was not that different in the film world of that time either. Film people talked only about the movies.

Ravi Shankarji keeps coming up in our discussions—because he was the only person I knew then who could talk on any subject. Whenever we travelled together by plane, he would buy ten magazines at the airport—newspapers, magazines on fashion or film, *Time, Newsweek* or whatever—and read them all during the flight. I started doing that too. I learned much more about language through reading than I had learned at school.

NMK: Do you still read a lot?

ZH: Absolutely. I read novels, newspapers and magazines. I read books on people in sports, in cricket, for example. I like reading but I guess I'm basically an escapist and so I usually read fiction. I like the Foundation series by the American science-fiction writer Isaac Asimov. Those are my favourite.

NMK: What about biographies of musicians? Do they interest you?

ZH: I have read books on Miles Davis, John Coltrane and Charlie 'Bird' Parker. They are considered biographies, but the musicians themselves were not involved. The books were written after the subject had passed away, so I don't know how much of Miles Davis's own thinking was in his biography.

Ravi Shankarji, on the other hand, was involved in his book, *My Music, My Life*, from the first till the very last page. Everything that's there you know was written under his watchful eye. He talked about his life and his music and it was clearly all him.

I recently read Roger Federer's biography, but it felt more about the guy who wrote it and what he thought of this great tennis player. Sure, the writer talked about Federer's forehand and backhand and stuff like that, but I found nothing about how Federer saw life. Sometimes that happens with biographies.

NMK: Did you find that frustrating?

ZH: I think it's misleading and not necessarily frustrating. My wife Toni gave me the book because she knows I am a Roger Federer fan. That's why I read it.

I'm a little apprehensive about biographies that do not involve the subject. If you read Muhammad Ali's book, *The Greatest: My Own Story*, you can visualize Ali saying those things and you can hear his voice. For example, our conversation involves me, and the reader will know that.

NMK: And poetry? Do you enjoy poetry?

ZH: I like poetry. But reading it needs time. I like the idea of reading a Faiz couplet and trying to understand where the poet is going with it. I like Dylan Thomas, Keats and Wordsworth. T.S. Eliot is very good, but I think I prefer Urdu poetry.

I grew up around Urdu poets, and so there is some peripheral insight into that tradition. When Majrooh Sultanpuri Sahib says, '*Saari duniya mujhe kehti tera saudai hai, ab mera hosh mein aana teri ruswai hai*' [The whole world says that I have lost all reason because of you, if I were now to regain my sanity it would bring disgrace upon you], I think I understand the feelings behind his words.

NMK: What language do you consider your language today? Is it Urdu or English? For example, what language do you dream in?

ZH: Ah! For the first eighteen years of my life it was probably Urdu and the following few years it was very confused, and now it's mostly English. I find that if I have to give an interview in Hindi or Urdu, it takes me a short while to become fluent again. I am translating from English and that's because I speak English all the time. Many Indians I know also speak to me in English.

For the most part, I think I dream in English. When I dream of my father and mother or other people who decide to join the dream, it's in Urdu, the language that I remember them by. When it is just a dream, it's in English.

NMK: People say when we're angry or sad we revert to a language in which expressing our emotions comes naturally. That language could be our mother tongue.

ZH: If you have lived a life which has defined parameters, you usually revert to a particular language. But when you have a life like mine which is all over the place, I suppose it's different. I have found myself at home in Bombay talking to Shaukat Apa, who looks after our home, in Urdu—it just comes out automatically, and then I switch to English a few minutes later.

NMK: I think personalities change when people express themselves in different languages. Would you agree?

ZH: Yes, it's a whole personality change. When I talk to Vikkuji [T.H. Vinayakram], the South Indian ghatam player, I speak to him in a South Indian tone. It's not only the words but also the voice levels change. It is very interesting to see it happen.

I was sitting in the living room the other day, here in Bombay, and my sister, Khurshid Apa, who is visiting from London, was talking on the phone to someone in another city in India and her voice rose about eight decibels! Her voice automatically went up. I told her: 'Khurshid Apa, there is no need to shout. They can hear you very clearly. This is not an old phone!' [*smiles*]

NMK: You said you grew up among poets. Do they still count among the people that you meet in India?

ZH: I enjoy meeting Javed Akhtar Sahib because the conversation invariably turns to music or poetry. It is not surprising that his views on poetry would be enlightening, but his insights on music came as a surprise to me.

I did not have a close connection with Kaifi Azmi Sahib and Majrooh Sultanpuri Sahib. I saw them when I was playing rhythms for a film song by Roshanji and then by O.P. Nayyarji.

I did know that film lyricists were aware of rhythm, but I wondered if they knew about taal and rhythm cycles. What did metre mean to them? I could tell they knew all that, but I was never close enough to a poet to ask about the extent of their understanding.

Rind jo mujhko samajhte hain unhen hosh nahin
Maikada saaz hoon main maikada bardosh nahin

[Those who think I am a drunkard are not in their senses
I visit the tavern but do not carry it around with me]

This verse is by Jigar Moradabadi and my thought was—is this couplet in a particular rhythm cycle? Does that apply here? When I got to know Gulzar Sahib and Javed Sahib better, it was wonderful to discover they were complete rhythmists. It is amazing to see how the words they write fit rhythmically on the tune, how mathematically lined up their lyrics are.

Lyricists clearly have a total understanding of rhythm and rhythm cycles. Think of Raja Mehdi Ali Khan Sahib's '*Aap ki nazron ne samjha pyaar ke kaabil mujhe, dil ki ye dhadkan thehar jaa, mil gayi manzil mujhe.*' [Your eyes tell me that you think me worthy of being loved. O heart, do not beat so fast, now that I have found purpose in life.] What a beautiful song. As soon as I heard it, the seven-beat metre was obvious to me. The seven-beat metre goes like—*ta ra ta ta ta ra ta*—*ta* (one). '*Aap-ki-nazron-ne-samjha…*'

NMK: That's such a wonderful composition by Madan Mohan and how beautifully Lata Mangeshkar has sung it. I'd like to clarify—does the understanding of rhythm not come from the composer when the lyricist is writing to the tune?

ZH: Yes, when writing on a tune, but finding the right words that allow that rhythmic flow is where a great lyricist comes in. The words must have meaning and they should not sound robotic just because you need to get the rhythm right.

I think poets and lyricists are artists of the highest order. Some of them can also sing beautifully in tarannum. Javed Sahib does not sing in tarannum, but when he recites a line, you can hear the rhythm. When it comes to Gulzar Sahib, his writing does not indicate rhythm in a transparent way. But the verses have rhythm: '*Tu jo mera beta hota, main tujhe Pinocchio pukarta*' [If you were my son, I would call you Pinocchio].

We once worked on a project together, a dance musical called *Pinocchio*. It was performed in Delhi and I composed the songs, and Taufiq assisted me with the music. Gulzar Sahib's words were simple and clear, but for a moment I was stumped. I was teaching in Princeton at the time, and I called him up in Bombay. I said: 'Gulzar Sahib, just read the lines to me; don't sing, just read please.' When he read the lines to me, the melody and metre was clear and the rhythm was right there. So I wrote a tune on his words.

NMK: Your love of Urdu must be because it was the language you spoke at home. You said when you dream of your parents, they speak in Urdu. Did you talk to them in Urdu?

ZH: It was always in Urdu. The Urdu newspaper *Inquilab* was delivered to the house every morning and my father and mother would sit and read it over a cup of tea. They were fluent in Urdu but they spoke Punjabi at home. I do not speak much Punjabi. I used to hang out with my Hindi- and Urdu-speaking friends. The whole neighbourhood of Mahim spoke Urdu, because the majority of people living there were Muslims.

NMK: Your parents were clearly a big influence on you. Did you want to be like your father—not only in the way you played the tabla, but also in personality?

ZH: I have spoken about this many times. I understood at one point in my life that I should not try to be like my father. I realized this when I heard a comment Abba made to a friend of his. I was in my twenties, and had already played professionally for about thirteen years. I had even played with Abba on the stage. At the end of a concert, one of his friends said: 'Oh, that was so beautiful. You must be so proud. Your son plays exactly like you.' The friend meant it as a compliment, but Abba said: 'I hope he does not play like me because I have achieved what I had to.'

These were his words in Urdu: '*Mera toh ho gaya Ustad Allarakha, abhi doosra Ustad Allarakha toh copy hoga ... fayda kya hai? Main toh yeh dua karunga ke mera ladka mujhse achchha bajaaye, kuchh aur kare, kuchh naya kare, aage jaaye*' [My statement of music as Ustad Allarakha has my stamp on it. It is recognized. What's the point of my son doing the same thing? I pray he'll play better than me, do something new and different—take his playing forward].

Abba's words stuck in my head. At first I thought: 'Oh, he doesn't want me to be like him.' I felt a little sad and a little hurt, but it made sense when I understood why I enjoyed my father's tabla recordings, or the recordings of Kishan Maharajji, or Ahmedjaan Thirakwa Khansahib. Although Abba's guru, Mian Qadir Baksh, was one of the greatest legends of his time, I could hear that my father did not sound anything like Mian-ji. Abba was his own sound, his own expression and his own man. He had found his personal way of communicating and connecting, and had spent years developing those skills. That is why it was important for him that I should not be his carbon copy because copies get thrown in the waste bin. I had to find my own expression. It's like the five hundred singers who imitate Lata, Rafi, Mukesh or Kishore. They'll always remain imitations.

Though I admired the skills of great tabla players, I did not pay attention to something that was staring me in the face—the fact that each of them had their own voice—they were all different.

My father taught my two brothers, Fazal and Taufiq, and me, and also all his students, that we had to find our own style. He was very comfortable with the idea that his sons would not be like him—unlike many masters in India who are hell-bent on training their students to be in their image. He set us on a path on which we found ourselves musically and instilled in us the idea that it is not wrong to assimilate, analyse and emulate when necessary.

NMK: Your father seemed to have been open to many possibilities.

ZH: That's right, he was. That's why he could do so many different things. One of his early jobs was at All India Radio in Bombay, where he was employed as an A-grade classical singer, composer and tabla player. He sang playback for films, and had even sung for Prithviraj Kapoor.

As far as I know, in the early 1950s, Abba was the only Indian classical musician who composed for films. He used the name A.R. Qureshi for the screen and wrote music for about thirty-six Hindi movies, including films like *Sabak*, *Madari*, *Khandaan* and *Maa Baap*. Scoring for films made him a more complete musician, perhaps more so than some of his peers. In later years, the sarangi player Ram Narayanji, Shivkumar Sharmaji, Hariprasad Chaurasiaji, Rais Khansahib and other musicians also started working for films.

NMK: Was he attached to a particular film studio?

ZH: He was on the payroll of Mohan Studio and used to go there almost every day. The studio was quite far from our home in Mahim. When you got off the local train at Andheri, you had to take a little road going east—in those days it was a little road. You could see open fields, trees and forests for about a mile or two, and Mohan Studio was down that way. Further south was Natraj Studio, where Shakti Samantaji and other film-makers had their offices. Many film-makers worked in Andheri. In fact, Mohan Studio used to be called the K. Asif Studio and that was where the famous Sheesh Mahal set in *Mughal-e-Azam* was built and the song '*Jab pyaar kiya toh darna kya*' was shot.

NMK: Bimal Roy had his offices at Mohan Studio as well.

ZH: Yes, I believe so. Did I tell you that I auditioned for young Prince Salim's role in *Mughal-e-Azam*? The role that eventually went to Jalal Agha.

My father and Asif Sahib knew each other well. The famous Kathak dancer Sitara Deviji was his first wife, and Abba and she were friends. My father had accompanied her on the tabla many times. I am sure you know that Asif Sahib's second wife, Nigar Sultana, played the role of Bahaar in *Mughal-e-Azam*.

NMK: Yes. What do you remember of the audition?

ZH: Abba's Man Friday, Shaukat, took me to Mohan Studio one day. Shaukat has passed away now. Besides working for my father, he would moonlight as a film extra. So Shaukat took me to see Asif Sahib because he had asked Abba to send me over. I remember they were filming on the Sheesh Mahal set, and I met Dilip Kumar Sahib there. He looked at me, cupped his hands around my face and lifted my chin so that he could take a closer look. He turned to Shaukat and said: '*Asif ke paas le jaana*' [Take him to Asif]. So that was that. It was hardly a real audition. I don't think there were proper auditions in those days. Someone just looked at an aspiring actor and said: '*Isko le lete hain*' [Let's take him]. No one used to ask the actor to read lines or anything like that. That's not how it was done.

Asif Sahib and his team gave me a toffee and asked me to go and play while they talked. I don't know what the outcome was but apparently my father had a change of heart and said: '*Nahin, yeh actor nahin banega, yeh music karega, musician hoga*' [No, he will not become an actor, he'll play music and become a musician].

NMK: I interviewed the composer Naushad Ali in 1988 and he told me how he managed to get Bade Ghulam Ali Khan to sing in *Mughal-e-Azam* for the now famous love scene between Salim and Anarkali. Naushad Sahib seemed to suggest that classical musicians had to be persuaded to sing in films. Did you sense a divide between the classical music world and the film world?

ZH: No. I don't like putting things into slots and I'm glad the seriousness of being a classical musician was not imposed on me as a young man.

NMK: But, of course, your father was composing for films—so that divide did not occur to him either. I know that Ali Akbar Khan played the sarod for the famous Lata Mangeshkar song '*Suno chhoti si gudiya ki lambi kahaani*' from the film *Seema*. Do you remember the other songs with his contribution?

ZH: He played the sarod for '*O jaanewaale ruk ja koi dam*' in Bimal Roy's *Devdas*, and composed music for other films, including Chetan Anand's *Aandhiyan*, Merchant/Ivory's first film, *The Householder*, Satyajit Ray's *Devi* and Tapan Sinha's *Hungry Stones*.

I believe that Ali Akbar Khansahib enjoyed that part of his life because it was a creative process which required a different way of thinking and involved people who were interesting—film people were not like some of the old ustads and gurus, paan-chewing and talking in a certain way. It was a whole different world and it was a lot of fun for him. Film songs also meant playing short pieces, following the tune, enhancing the words as much as possible to bring out their meaning—it's a challenge to say a lot in a short piece.

NMK: We must talk about Jaidev, Ali Akbar Khan's former student. His sarod playing and compositions were stunning. I am thinking of his extraordinary songs in *Hum Dono*.

ZH: Just like our former neighbour and the other great composer, Sajjad Hussain Sahib, Jaidev Sahib had the reputation of being difficult to work with.

Jaidev Sahib was one of the best composers Hindi cinema has ever had. His songs were off the beaten track. He preferred to compose on the lyrics, so that he could give the words the right musical shape. Think of Sahir's *'Main zindagi ka saath nibhaata chala gaya'* [I have flowed with what life offers me]. The words have the proper melodic intonation. I just don't know from where Jaidev Sahib got that talent, because you have to know poetry well. He composed amazing songs in *Hum Dono, Mujhe Jeene Do* and *Reshma aur Shera*.

Hum Dono was one of those films where the music, direction, photography, the acting, everything just came together. When all the stars align, you get a great movie. It has one of the greatest bhajans ever written, *'Allah tero naam'*. Another beautiful song that I like is *'Raat bhi hai kuchh bheegi bheegi'* from *Mujhe Jeene Do*.

Jaidev Sahib studied the sarod with Ali Akbar Khansahib. When the latter came to Bombay and was composing music for Chetan Anand's *Aandhiyan*, Jaidev Sahib was his assistant. When Khansahib moved on from Navketan, Jaidev Sahib continued working there and became S.D. Burman's assistant. Kudos to Chetan Sahib, Dev Sahib and Sunil Dutt Sahib for asking him to write music for their films. I truly believe that Jaidev Sahib was an underrated genius.

There was also Roshanji whose songs in *Barsaat ki Raat, Taj Mahal*, etc., were big hits, but he was not given due recognition either. Neither was Madan Mohanji. Many music directors of that era were exceptional composers and knew a lot about Indian music.

NMK: The current generation of music lovers adore the three composers that you have just mentioned: Jaidev, Roshan and Madan Mohan. I think their work is appreciated even more so today. Their compositions have a gentle melodic feel that never overwhelms the words, and yet have tunes you can never forget.

When did your father stop composing for films? And why?

ZH: Do you remember that we talked about the time when I was born and when my father was very ill? Well, Abba started to get well; this was sometime in 1954 or '55, and that's when he decided to stop working for films. His first love was always the tabla and the Indian classical music world, and he was flooded with offers for concert work. Many musicians wanted him to accompany them. So Abba started doing that.

When he was at Mohan Studio, he had to work there every day. But if he played on the stage, it involved only about twelve days a month. On top of that, he could make ten times the money that he made as a film composer. So, for about ten years, he toured all around the world with Ravi Shankarji. They went everywhere, including Japan and Europe.

NMK: So was it your mother, Bavi Begum, who looked after the family?

ZH: Yes, she looked after the house and us. My mother was very forward-thinking and more grounded than Abba. She wanted her children to be educated—even though she herself could not speak English. Most of the children in Mahim were sent to madrasas to study the Quran. But Amma had a very different vision of our future. She made sure that my sisters, Khurshid Apa and Razia Apa, studied in an Urdu-medium school, the Anjuman-e-Islam, whereas most girls in the Muslim community in our area, especially in the 1950s, were uneducated.

I was the only kid in the whole neighbourhood, for example, who went to an English-medium school, St Michael's High School. I don't know why but Amma felt that I must study English and it was she who made sure that I attend school every day. She used to argue with Abba and insist: *'Nahi, usko school jaane do, bahut ho gaya riyaaz, usko padhai karne do'* [No more, let him go to school. Enough practice, he must study].

Abba's family was not educated and he was not particularly keen about my schooling. He would tell my mother: *'Arey tu usko kyun school bhej rahi hai? Woh toh tabla bajaayega, usko riyaaz karne do. School mein jaa ke kya karega?'* [Why are you sending him to school? He's going to play the tabla. Let him practice. Why waste time at school?]

At one stage, Amma even sent me to stay with a very dear friend of hers so that I would be away from my father's influence and study instead of playing the tabla. It was crazy. I was under fifteen, in the ninth or tenth standard, when Amma thought I had to focus on my studies, so I was sent to the home of Bibi Bai Almas. I lived there for about a year.

The intriguing thing about Bibi Bai Almas was her lineage. She had African ancestry and her family had settled in Hyderabad and Gujarat. She came from a more liberal kind of an Islamic background and because of that she had even acted in some early stunt films. She did not change her name for the screen and was known as Bibi Bai Almas. I have not seen any of her movies because she had retired by the time I was sent to stay with her. Her daughter Habiba Rahman is now working as a film choreographer.

NMK: What a small world! I interviewed Habiba Rahman in the early 1990s for a documentary series that I was making for Channel 4. She seemed lovely.

ZH: She is. We grew up together. Habiba was learning Kathak from Sitara Deviji and Bibi Almas was also teaching dance. Some of her dance students would come for lessons to Bibi's house, so I played the tabla for them. It turned out to be a blessing in disguise, and came in handy when I ended up playing for great dancers like Sitara Deviji and Birju Maharajji. I was already familiar with the material.

I remember Bibi Bai was very strict. We had to be up at five in the morning—anyway I was used to getting up early—we would say our namaz, read the Quran, have breakfast and get ready for school.

NMK: You said you were used to waking up early. Can you describe a typical day when you were say ten or twelve and living at home with your parents?

ZH: My father would wake me up at 3 a.m. He sat with me like we're sitting now, and he would teach me vocally. We didn't play. We just sang rhythms (bols/rhythmic syllables), back and forth. He would tell me this composition is by this master or that master. You could see the devotion on his face in the way that he spoke about the old masters. It was touching and, thanks to him, I developed a deep reverence for music and a deep respect for the old masters.

That's how we spent the hours between three and six in the morning. Then my mother would pull me away from him, give me breakfast and send me to the madrasa to study the Quran.

Across the street from the madrasa was St Michael's High School, and I would head there. We sang hymns at assembly and then we'd go to our classrooms.

I had lunch at school and came home at around three in the afternoon. I practised what my father had taught me that morning and when I had finished practising, I played with some friends in the neighbourhood. Then I'd come home, do my homework, eat and off to bed at about 10 p.m. That was more or less my daily routine.

NMK: If you woke up at 3 a.m., that means you had only five hours sleep—not very much for a growing child.

ZH: That's about all I got. Five hours. I'm catching up on sleep now. [*both laugh*]

NMK: Were you a happy kid?

ZH: I think I was quite happy. I was asked if I really wanted to study the tabla. And it's only when Abba saw my interest had become an obsession that he started getting me up at three in the morning. I mean how many kids get to hang out with their dads? I didn't see many kids in the neighbourhood hanging out with their fathers. Their dads were hanging around the paanwala's shop, enjoying a smoke. Most kids spent time playing because they did not have anything to do. At least I had things to do. There was purpose from a very young age.

NMK: Where was the family home in Mahim?

ZH: For the first three-and-a-half years of my life, we all lived in one room that had no toilet. We had to use the common toilets. It was a chawl. The building does not exist anymore.

In 1954, we managed to upgrade to a flat in Akram Terrace, which is behind the dargah in Mahim. Akram Terrace still exists. It was thanks to my mother, who was very frugal, that we could move from the chawl.

Amma could make one rupee go a long way and in those days one rupee did go a long way. She managed to pay the deposit and the rent on the Akram Terrace ground-floor flat. It had two medium-sized rooms on either side of a large living room. There was a small kitchen, a bathroom and toilet. That was our home till we moved to Simla House in the late 1960s—to this same flat, where we're now talking. Coming here was a big graduation.

NMK: How did your mother manage to buy this place?

ZH: It cost about 124,000 rupees; a fortune in the 1960s. All the money had to be paid in cash and upfront. Mortgages and bank loans were not possible and in those days it was all hard cash.

Amma had saved up as much as she could. Back then you could transfer your pagdi to another tenant and, if I remember right, she got about 55,000 rupees from the deposit of the Akram Terrace flat, but we were still short of some thousands. So Amma spoke to the session musicians that she knew and asked them to find me work playing the tabla for film music so that I could earn a little money. And so I ended up playing the tabla on many film songs—songs that were composed by a variety of music directors, including Naushad Sahib, Roshanji, and Madan Mohanji, and there were others too. This was sometime in the mid-1960s. I was only a teenager. Whatever

I earned was added to our savings, and Amma finally managed to buy this flat in Simla House. All this happened when my father was out of India on tour. He had left while we were still in Mahim and when he returned we were living on Nepean Sea Road. It must have been a shock for him to come back to an entirely new home.

I must admit those days are a blur now. For two months, I would go to school during the first half of the day, and the second half would find me in some recording studio. Some of my tabla player friends recognize my playing and try to jog my memory: 'What about this song? And this? Is this you?'

I can't remember the songs very well. There was Madan Mohanji's music in *Mera Saaya*. S.D. Burman's *Guide* and *Dr Vidya*. There were lots of films in production and I played alongside the session musicians; many were from Goa. There was Mr D'Costa, Mr Waghmare, Mr Fernandes, a Parsi guy called Guddi and of course young Kersi Lord. He passed away recently. There was also Lala Bhai, Sattar Bhai, Naidu the dholki player, Maruti Keer, Karim and Iqbal—they were great players of the tabla, dholak, dholki and various other drums. I remember we did not call the musicians by their first names because you showed respect.

Back then I think there were about four or five recording studios used for film music. There was the Bombay Sound Service, which was part of the Bombay Labs near the Portuguese Church in Dadar, and Mehboob Recording Studio was in Bandra. It had a big hall for musicians to sit and play. We also recorded at Famous and Film Center—both studios were in Tardeo. At Mohan Studio, they would record music on their sound stage after the day's shoot had taken place. That's why in the old days, they used to tell the musicians: '*Set pe paisa milta hai*' [You'll get paid on the set].

The sound engineers ran the recording studios. They were not brought in for a particular film. The in-house sound recordist at Bombay Sound Labs was B.N. Sharma. Minoo Katrak, the sound designer, mixer and recording engineer, worked at Famous in Tardeo. They were very well known. The recording engineer Daman Sood came later.

Nowadays composers can sample everything. They have a big keyboard on which they have violins, violas, cellos, trumpets, the French horn, etc. Depending on the budget, the composer uses what's on the sequencer. They call in singers who will record the song without the orchestra. The singers just have the sur [a pitch instrument] and, based on their rendition, the orchestra is then created and the song is cut: '*Ye mukhda hoga, ye antara hoga*' [this is the mukhda, this is the antara].

Even the singers do not know how their songs will eventually sound. If the song needs a flute or sarangi, they'll call a musician. If the song is a rhythmic kind of song, they might call a dholkiwala, a dholwala. But the main orchestral sound is from sequencing.

Back then we used to record on mono tracks, which meant all the musicians were recorded on one track and the voice on another. The recording engineers were marvellous. They used to set up four microphones and the sound of many instruments went into this one input that would be mixed on the fly. '*Yahaan flute ka solo aanewala hai*' [The flute solo comes here] and then in the next antara, there's the sitar piece. The placement of the mics was precisely worked out, so when it was the turn of the sitar player, he could be heard. The sound recordists knew the volume of which instrument had to be increased and when to do so.

I remember seeing Hariprasad Chaurasiaji standing at a microphone and around him sat a santoor player and a sarangi player. When the tune needed the flute, Hariprasadji took a small step towards the mic and played. Once his piece was done, he stepped back. That's how it was done.

There were not many rhythm players, as far as I can recall. There was a dholak player who sat opposite me on the same level and a khanjariwala and manjirawala would sit nearby. We had a mic hanging over us and, during the rehearsals, we were told: '*Arey woh aap ka bayan baraabar nahin aa raha hai, thoda aise baithiye. Zara bajaana, achchha woh chanti theek nahin aa rahi hai, zara sa aage aaiye.*' [We can't hear the bass tabla clearly, just move a little. Now play. We can't hear the chanti, the high end of the tabla. Please come forward.] The Indian sound engineers were very knowledgeable about film music and the musical instruments. They knew how they should sound and how to record them correctly.

The soloists in big bands in America also stand up when playing and then sit down once their piece is over—by doing this, they create the sound balance.

Nowadays we have multi-track recording and every bit of sound can be corrected—you can fix the tune, the pitch and whatever else you need to fix. It's an entirely different process, but in the old days, the only person who could be re-recorded, with the least hassle that is, was the singer because he or she had been recorded on a separate mic.

NMK: I must share an insightful and telling quote about Lata Mangeshkar by Meena Kumari, who said: 'If Lataji is singing, we don't need to act.'

ZH: Because Lataji has already done everything! She has a three-minute song, and I have a one-hour concert, so I have time. The idea of projecting the whole ball of wax in a short amount of time is something very special. What's important is the understanding of language, and the singer's diction and ability to interpret the words in their many shades. When Lata Mangeshkar sang *'Mora nadaan balma na jaane dil ki baat'* [My naive lover does not understand the ways of the heart], she had eight seconds to create emotion in that line. She is not thinking about it, she's just doing it. Her remarkable ability was to interpret and express those feelings and sing in a manner that, when Madhubala or Nargis parted their lips, the song appeared as though coming from them.

For me the heart of a good song are the words. They convey what the character is feeling and give expression to the emotions. This makes creating melodies on those words even more challenging. No one was as good as Majrooh Sahib in writing lyrics on pre-composed melodies. His words were beautiful, simple and straightforward—just what the tune needed.

Take Majrooh Sahib's song *'Mehboob mere mehboob mere, tu hai to duniya kitni haseen hai, jo tu nahin toh kuchh bhi nahin hai'* [My beloved, the world is full of splendour because of you, without you there is emptiness]. It's beautiful. I remember that was one of Abba's favourite songs. I asked him why, and he said the words fitted the simplicity of the melody perfectly and that it all came together effortlessly.

Sahir Sahib also wrote on the tune, but it did not work as well. But think of his wonderful '*Aadmi ko chahiye waqt se darr kar rahe, kaun jaane kis ghadi waqt ka badle mizaaj*' [Man should fear Time, who knows when its temperament will change].

In the early days, the directors and the composers were knowledgeable about Urdu.

Many of today's film composers have grown up in an English-speaking environment and therefore are not that close to Hindi–Urdu traditions. That said, it's difficult for me to comment about the lyricists and composers today because I have not seen the recent films. I know that some people have worked as musicians in their formative years and are now composers, like Shankar–Ehsaan–Loy, A.R. Rahman, Salim–Suleiman, Jatin–Lalit, and Aadesh Srivastava, who just passed away. They used to be rhythm players, piano players and guitarists. Of the older generation, Laxmikantji was a mandolin player and Pyarelalji a violinist before they became composers. R.D. Burman was a tabla and rhythm player. Composers who start off as musicians are definitely more experienced at scoring for films.

We must remember that ultimately composers have to provide music according to the director's brief and compose a soundtrack that works within the narrative of the film. So, some of it will not be their best work, and the composers will

Just married. 23 September 1978. St. Joseph's Church, Bronxville, NY. With Judy Lynn, maid of honour. Photograph: Joseph Squillante

With Toni and Toni's mother, Angela Minnecola. Wedding celebration, Eastchester, NY. 23 September 1978. Photograph: Joseph Squillante

Nikah. San Anselmo, California. 11 November 1978. Toni and Zakir with Abbaji (Ustad Allarakha) looking on. Imam conducting the ceremony partially hidden.

(*left to right*) Abbaji, Anisa in Toni's arms and Ammaji (Zakir Hussain's mother Bavi Begum). Los Angeles. September 1983.

George Harrison on an unexpected visit to Simla House to see the Allarakha family. Bombay, c. mid-1970s.

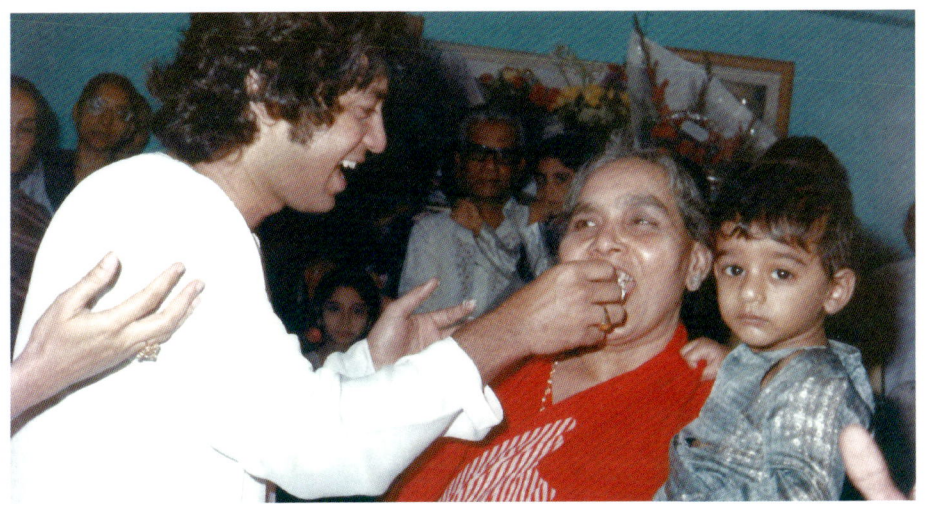

Celebrating Zakir Hussain's birthday was a family ritual. Seen here with his mother Bavi Begum. In her arms is sister Razia's son, Ehetsham, who passed away in 2016. Simla House, Bombay. 1983.

With Abbaji and sister Razia. Simla House, Bombay. Date unknown.

With (*left to right*) Shobha Gurtu, Abbaji and Pandit Dinkar Kaikini. Simla House, Bombay. Date unknown.

(*left to right*) Anisa, Isabella, Zakir and Toni at the Taj Mahal, Agra, one of the few trips to the Taj. January 1996. Zakir himself drove the family to Agra from New Delhi and onto Fatehpur Sikri.

A Kathak teacher and dancer, Antonia Minnecola is seen here at Yoshi's Jazz Club at Moment Records' release party for the CD *Zakir Hussain and the Rhythm Experience*. Oakland, California. Summer 1993.

With *(left to right)* Selvaganesh, John McLaughlin and U. Srinivas (*Remember Shakti*). Bangalore. 2002.

Among the world's leading guitarists, John McLaughlin has been a close friend for many decades. Bangalore. 2002.

With Ustad Sultan Khan, the sarangi maestro with whom ZH has played numerous concerts over the years.

First album cover with Pandit Shivkumar Sharma. Zakir Hussain considers Shivji among his early mentors. Early 1980s. Photograph: Dhiraj Chawla

With (*left to right*) music director Tafo, Pandit Shivkumar Sharma and Nusrat Fateh Ali Khan. Bombay, mid-1990s. Photograph: Khurshid Aulia

President Abdul Kalam presenting Zakir Hussain with a post-concert token of appreciation (c. 2008-09). Zakir Hussain was awarded the Padma Bhushan, the third-highest civilian award in India, in 2002.

With daughter Anisa in front of the shop in Mahim, Bombay, where Zakir had his first professional photo taken. December 2010. Photograph: Elizabeth Phillips

Daughters Isabella Qureshi and Anisa Phillips.

Daughter Anisa and Taylor Phillips on their honeymoon. Udaipur. January 2011.

With Charles Lloyd and Herbie Hancock (*right*). Monterey, California. September 2014.
Photograph: Antonia Minnecola

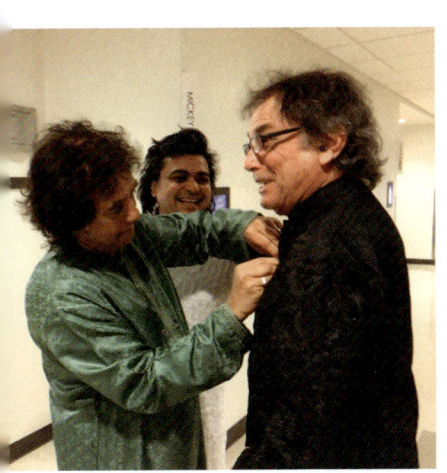

Gifting good friend Mickey Hart a kurta and helping him with the buttons as they get ready for the concert at Weill Hall, Green Music Center, Rohnert Park, California. Sitarist Niladri Kumar looks on. 30 October 2016.
Photograph: Antonia Minnecola

Founding members of the Alla Rakha Foundation at the Nehru Centre, London, 2001. With (*left to right*) Ismail Merchant, Ayub Aulia and sister Khurshid Aulia.
Photograph: Madan Arora

Zakir Hussain gave a surprise birthday concert along with Ustad Sultan Khan and his son Sabir Khan to celebrate the fiftieth birthday of film-maker/friend Sumantra Ghosal (*right*). Bombay. Photograph courtesy: Equinox Films

Jennifer Kapoor Memorial Concert with Louiz Banks (piano), Abhinav Khokar (bass), Avishai Cohen (trumpet) and Sanjay Divecha (guitar) at Prithvi Theatre, Bombay. 28 February 2017. Photograph courtesy: Kunal Kapoor

With Toni. Nikah Anniversary. San Anselmo, California. 11 November 2016.
Photograph: Isabella Qureshi

Cape Town, South Africa. December 2016.
Photograph: Rakesh Chaurasia

With Rakesh Chaurasia on train from Nice to Paris. Masters of Percussion tour. Summer 2015.

Train station in Nice. With (*left to right*) Deepak Bhatt, Abbos Kosimov, Mujeeb Dadarkar, Vijay Chauhan and Sabir Khan. Masters of Percussion tour. Summer 2015. Photograph: Rakesh Chaurasia

With (*left to right*) Chris Potter, Sanjay Divecha, Shankar Mahadevan, Louiz Banks and Dave Holland. CrossCurrents tour. Early 2017.

At home in San Anselmo, preparing his tabla for a tour. June 2015.
Photograph: Antonia Minnecola

With granddaughter Zara when she was five days old, at Anisa and Taylor's home in Los Angeles. 5 July 2015. Photograph: Isabella Qureshi

With granddaughter Zara.
Photograph: Antonia Minnecola

With granddaughter Zara. Zakir Hussain's workshop, Sukhasiddhi Foundation, Fairfax, California. August 2016. Photograph: Anisa Phillips

Zakir Hussain describes sound engineer Mujeeb Dadarkar as someone who has understood perfectly how to project the sound of Indian instruments all the way from the audience in the first row to the back row. Weill Hall, Green Music Center, Rohnert Park, California. 30 October 2016. Photograph: Antonia Minnecola

With (*left to right*) Ranjit Barot, Sridhar Parthasarathy, Kadambari Desai, Salim, Shikharnaad Qureshi, Taufiq Qureshi, Yogesh Samsi, Niladri Kumar, Geetika Varde Qureshi. (*Back row*): Mujeeb Dadarkar, Dhafer Youssef and his wife Shiraz Youssef. Simla House, Bombay. December 2014.

Royal Festival Hall, London. Photograph: Khurshid Aulia

Every year Zakir Hussain holds a retreat where he mentors over fifty tabla students. Sukhasiddhi Foundation, Fairfax, California. July 2015. Photograph: Antonia Minnecola

be the first to admit it. But what's interesting is that a composer like A.R. Rahman or the guys that I have mentioned, can still manage to insert at least one gem of a song into a film. That song will show their pedigree as composers and what they could do if they were given half the chance.

NMK: During the time your father was composing film music, did you meet any of the lyricists he was working with?

ZH: One day when I came home from school, Amma asked me not to make a noise because my father was working. I peeped into the room where Abba was sitting at the harmonium. There was a gentleman with a pen and paper in his hand who was sitting near Abba. When I looked closely, I realized it was the poet/lyricist Kaifi Azmi Sahib. So they sat there—tune, words, words and tune—all that was going on. They smiled at each other and, from time to time, they would ask Amma for some tea. They worked in that closed room for a long time and came up with a song.

One day I was telling Shabana Azmi, the poet's daughter, about this and I said: 'As a child I remember seeing your father in our Mahim home. I don't remember the song Abba and he were working on, but I think the film never got completed and was finally shelved.' I told Shabanaji the song went something like '*Main toh khwaja ki deewani hoon*' [I am obsessed with the Lord]. She said: 'You're fibbing, it can't be!' I asked why. 'My father was a communist; he would never write lines like that.'

But it was true, Kaifi Sahib needed work in those days and writing for films earned him money, so he could have been following a director's brief.

NMK: Do you think your father liked working for films?

ZH: Abba enjoyed composing, but he belonged to a very different era of music directors. In his time, he composed the music, the lyricist wrote the words, and together they presented the finished song to the director. The director did not tell them to add this line and that rhythm. It was very difficult for Abba to accept that some guy who knew nothing about music was telling him the kind of music he should compose. I remember hearing that the star of a film wanted his songs to be sung by a particular singer and my father put his foot down and said, sorry, no. Abba was that kind of a guy and so he gained the reputation of not playing ball.

I was aware that some actors, including Dilip Kumar, Dev Anand and Ashok Kumar, were knowledgeable about music, and so were some of the great directors, like K. Asif, Bimal Roy and Raj Kapoor. In fact, I recorded some songs for a Raj Kapoor film and, from my personal experience, I could see that he knew about music. Of course, there were other film-makers who knew about music, but I did not know them personally.

NMK: In 1989-90, I met the gifted composer Sajjad Hussain, whom you mentioned, and, like your father, he was clearly a man who did not compromise. You said he was your former neighbour in Mahim. Was he living close to your family?

ZH: Yes, if this is the building where we were—slightly off the main road—you walked to the main road and carried down a block and a half, and you'd find the Natal Building. That's where Sajjad Sahib lived. The building is still there. One of Lataji's gurus, Amaan Ali Khansahib, also lived in that building.

Sajjad Sahib was an uncompromising composer like Abba and Jaidev Sahib. They were vigilant about their work and proud of their music, and refused to change it in ways that did not fit their sensibilities. Sajjad Sahib wrote beautiful film songs that were challenging for a singer, and therefore more enjoyable, but he was not a team player and ultimately that's what film-making is all about. You're working with a director who has a vision of the complete movie in his head. You have to help him or her to create that film—you can't impose your vision on someone else's film. So, if they wanted an old-world sound, they did not ask Sajjad Sahib but went to Khayyam Sahib because he was easier to work with.

NMK: When you were playing the tabla for film songs, did you observe how the singers prepared for a recording?

ZH: Yes, I did. When a composer sat with Lata Mangeshkar, he sang her the tune on the harmonium, and she made some markings on the lyrics that she had previously written out in her own hand. Her markings created a map of the route that she was going to take through the song. That route highlighted certain notes, or which part of the song allowed her to take a breath—this line is this long, so I need to take a breath somewhere here—this is shorter, so that's not a problem. Lataji marked up her lyrics in a few minutes. The whole city was there: the water stops, the lunch stop and where she would take a break. It was all laid out. It's an incredible skill, and I know the singers of today use the same method too. The interesting thing is that this system of mapping is not standardized. All the singers have their own way of marking up the lyrics.

I also noticed that the composer rarely had to sing the song twice for playback singers; once was usually enough. They grasped the tune very quickly and were ready to record—this applied to many singers of the past like Lataji or Ashaji, but also to the current generation, including Sonu Nigam. They can sing the whole song straight through because they have mapped it all out and so follow the route and arrive at their destination.

NMK: Do you map your performance before a concert?

ZH: There's a difference because I am improvising, but I do work out an outline. Within the parameters, I'll navigate my way through, as and how I please. It's like being in a skating rink, you can go this way or that, or cut across, but you're still in the rink.

For me it's improvising—and that's not so difficult. But playback singers have to understand the meaning of the words and grasp the tune that has been sung by a composer who himself may not be a very good singer, and who may not have conveyed all the subtle nuances of the melody.

NMK: Is there such a thing as purity in film music?

ZH: [*irritated*] Purity? That's something I cannot come to terms with. If you're doing film music, it is already a non-Indian form and you're probably going to use Western instruments to play that music, so the concept of purity does not apply.

Take a composer like Sajjad Hussain Sahib. He was a fantastic mandolin player. I once heard him play with Abba in a house in Chowpatty—the way he played the mandolin, a small instrument like that, and for three hours. It was amazing to hear him. He was a superb musician. Sajjad Sahib's three sons also play the mandolin. But when you speak of 'purity', remember the mandolin is not an Indian instrument. It is a European instrument, related to other instruments such as the lute and the oud. In any case, it is totally non-Indian. So film music has been played and continues to be played on a variety of instruments that are not all purely Indian.

NMK: We have talked about recording film music, what about the process of recording classical music? Say, here in India or in the West.

ZH: That's straightforward. It doesn't really matter whether you're recording in India or in the US; it's the same process.

What's become increasingly problematic in India is to find a studio that has enough physical space for two or three musicians to sit together and play. Because it's all on the sequencer, there is no longer any need for large halls. The music director sits in the same room as the soundboard and there is a small booth for the soloist or singer. This small booth is the only space available for musicians, so that's a problem. Yash Chopra's YRF Studio has a large room for musicians and there are a few other recording studios in Bombay and in Madras. Mehboob Recording Studio had a large hall but it has closed down.

Recording gets complex when you're playing a different style of music, say, jazz; otherwise, recording a raga with a lead instrumentalist is no different from a performance. When we make a sixty-minute CD, it takes about a day. And if something goes wrong, you don't have to repeat the entire piece because you can cut and edit and do all that. In the old days, a recording of a two-hour concert had to be edited down to forty minutes—remember, an LP had only twenty minutes on each side? That was a big challenge because the music had to have completion and resolution, and the edits could not sound jarring.

I enjoy recording. It's a creative process—it's like going to the beach with an easel and canvas to paint the scene. You look at the horizon, the shades of the clouds, the sunset—and ignore the pollution. [*both laugh*]

The power of shaping things is the fun of recording. I can start off with one thought and end up with an entirely different one. In the old days, the one thought was the only thought and did not become anything else. To take the same clay pot and create different shapes is like waving a magic wand.

NMK: Was working on film music a good period in your life?

ZH: You must remember I was still in my teens, and somewhat taken by the glamour of cinema. I grew up on films; I listened to film songs and enjoyed them. To be part of the process was very exciting, to see how film music was put together was a whole new world to me. It felt as though you had entered a large hall and walked up to a gigantic screen and stepped into it. Here's this car chase scene, and you were right there, sitting in the back seat. Some months later, when I would see the film and hear the background music, I smiled, knowing that I was a part of it.

NMK: Many people love the idea of a list of top tens. Do you have a favourite Hindi film song?

ZH: It is kind of hard to say because there are so many categories of film songs: sad songs, romantic songs, happy songs, and qawwalis—I have listened to quite a few songs. How to pick a favourite?

Many composers and lyricists have written fabulous songs. Sometimes I am just sitting around and I remember a very beautiful song and I really love it. I forget about it and then another song comes to mind.

When someone would ask me to name my favourite song, I would say: 'Anything by Madan Mohanji is great.' Consciously or unconsciously, I was aware that I could not tie myself to one song because that meant I would be limiting my vision and emotional growth. It's like asking me which raga I like. There are a few ragas that I like very much. In the morning, I like listening to Lalit. In the evening, I like Shree.

There is this need for human beings to establish the number one. And it cannot be—music is not sports. It's not boxing, where you become the number one ranking boxer. It does not mean you're the best boxer around, it just means you are ranked number one at that point in time because you happen to have won a few more fights than someone else.

NMK: You said the days when you were working as a session musician as a teenager are somewhat of a blur. How did you manage to juggle school and work?

ZH: Did I tell you about Mr Sharma? He was my teacher and Abba's fan. He explained to Father Bento, the principal of my school, that he thought I was talented and should be allowed to play music.

A deal was struck, perhaps the first of its kind in a school in Bombay, where a kid could follow the school curriculum in his own way. Mr Sharma was the man who made it possible. He would leave my homework with Amma, I would go to the recording studio, and, when I came home, she would give me my homework. If I had to travel for a concert to Patna or Hyderabad, Aurangabad or Ahmedabad, I would study on the train under the reading light.

NMK: You started working at a very young age, as did your father in his time. I believe his family spoke Dogri as well as Punjabi and belonged to the Muslim Dogra community. Can you tell me something about the family?

ZH: They were originally from a village called Phagwal, on the border of Jammu and Punjab. Later they moved to Ramri by the river Raavi in Shakargarh. Ramri is now in Pakistan and it was there that my grandfather, who was called Hashim Ali Qureshi Sahib, had settled. The family lived in a spacious house surrounded by mango groves. To get to Ramri, you had to ride a horse on a dirt road. I don't know what it's like now. I have not been there in thirty years.

Essentially, Abba's family were farmers. I once started writing a book about him and the first line was: 'God made a mistake by having the stork bring my father to a farmer's home when it should have been a musician's home.' [*laughs*]

I know Abba was eleven or so when he ran away from home to stay with an uncle in Lahore. I don't know my great-uncle's name because Abba always referred to him as 'Chacha'. In Lahore, Abba did a menial job in a shop. Music was always

Abba's thing and perhaps that's why he went to Lahore because the city was a hub of cultural activity then and many musicians lived there.

Every Friday, after prayers, a baithak was held in someone's house. The Punjabi way of saying it was: '*Aaj unke takiye pe baithak hai.*' In other words, musicians would be performing in the sitting area of a private home. These baithaks took place in the afternoon because the musicians had to play for the baijis later that evening. One day, Abba's uncle took him to a baithak because he knew of my father's passion for music.

On that particular day, a Dhrupad singer was singing and his tabla player was unable to decipher the composition. So the host asked if there was another tabla player in the house who could play. Without realizing the enormity of the situation, or the protocol involved, Abba said he knew what to do, and so he went ahead. Everyone was amazed to see this young kid playing so well. Abba must have heard the composition somewhere and it had stuck in his mind.

One of the musicians at the baithak asked which ustad was training the young boy, and was told that he did not have a teacher, but was very keen on studying the tabla. The musician spoke of an ustad who belonged to the Punjab gharana and who lived in the same neighbourhood. He suggested that Abba's uncle should take his nephew there. That's how Abba met his guru, Mian Qadir Baksh, and when he did, my father was convinced that he had seen Mian-ji in his childhood.

NMK: I read an article on your father in which he said that he had seen his guru's face reflected in a river and so when, as a teenager, he met Mian Qadir Baksh, the master of the pakhawaj and tabla, he was sure this was the guru that he had been seeking. Is this true?

ZH: I try to explain these things rationally. There are certain powers at play but something like music is rooted in tradition, so you want to make sure that it's not all myth. There must be some reality attached, for it to be valid. That is very important to me.

It is possible that a musician passing through Abba's village might have showed him the guru's photograph in a newspaper. Someone could have been listening to the radio and said: 'Mian-ji is playing.' So his guru's name and face was somewhere at the back of Abba's mind and, when he met him, Abba felt he had seen his guru sometime earlier.

NMK: How did your father know how to play before that fateful day at the Lahore baithak?

ZH: Travelling musicians and nautankis used to perform in the village square in Abba's childhood. They were known as 'mirasis'. My father would watch the musicians, but his attention was on the tabla player and probably that's how he learned—by observation.

When Mian-ji was teaching Abba the tabla, it is clear to me that it was he who told him to learn singing as well. So Mian-ji sent Abba to Ashiq Ali Khansahib, who belonged to the Patiala gharana and who had also mentored Bade Ghulam Ali Khansahib. I think it was common for most rhythm players to know about vocal music because they had to understand what was expected of them when they were accompanying a singer, because singing was the top thing in those days. Instruments were not as much in vogue as they are now.

When Abba taught us, he would tell us about ragas and music compositions and talk about their emotional features, and how to support these compositions rhythmically. That was all part of the learning process.

NMK: In Mickey Hart's *Drumming at the Edge of Magic*, you have described the time that your father trained under Mian Qadir Baksh, in these words: 'Often the teacher was busy. Weeks would pass and then he wouldn't spend any time with my father, being busy with concerts or other students. But then he'd sit down with my father and for two or three days they'd do nothing but play the tabla together. In time, and with much practice, my father became a master.' Your father spent six years studying under his guru in Lahore. Was he working at the same time?

ZH: In 1936, when he was seventeen, Abba joined All India Radio (AIR) in Lahore. Because of his obvious talent, he was offered a job as a staff musician at AIR in Delhi in 1938. Two years later he was transferred to AIR, Bombay.

One day he decided to go back to his village and that's when he got married to my mother, who was from a village some distance away. It must have been an arranged marriage, though my father and mother were cousins. I don't know when they got married, but I think it was in the early 1940s. Abba found a place to stay in Bombay and my mother joined him.

You know I never once heard my mother call Abba by his name. She would say: *'Unko bulao'* [Call 'him'].

NMK: That was the tradition—a wife did not usually address her husband by name. I saw a charming thirty-minute black-and-white documentary titled *Allarakha*, made in 1970 by Chandrashekhar Nair of Films Division, in which your father said that twenty-five of the films in which he composed the music were hits and fifteen among these celebrated a fifty-week run, or what they called a golden jubilee hit in those days. In his interview, your father also proudly said that you were away in America at the time of filming. There was an evocative shot of your old Bakelite telephone with the number '359494'.

The short interview in the documentary with your mother was fascinating. She talked about how attached your father was to the family. It must have been hard on your mother, given that your father was away for months on end.

ZH: We were little kids, so the emotional stress that she must have felt was not obvious to me. I was busy playing cricket and hanging out. But I am very sure it was difficult for her because she had been thrown into this amazingly different life, from village to big city, and, by the time she had adjusted to it, her husband was off travelling around the world for five or six months at a stretch. Abba could read Urdu but not write it, so he had to find someone to write his letters for him. So letters were rare.

I once overheard Amma telling a friend—and it really stuck in my head—that she missed Abba a lot. There was nothing romantic about her comment—it was more about missing someone to talk with—just to have Abba around for support and advice.

NMK: When you were growing up, was money a problem? Or were you well off?

ZH: Oh no, we were poor. The big houses and big cars that we saw were in the movies. We would see well-dressed people arriving in their fancy cars to attend concerts. But I do not remember ever feeling: 'Oh, I want a car like that.' Many of my friends were living in homes that were far more modest than ours.

You must remember tabla players were on the lower rung of the hierarchy. The singer was the highest paid, the instrumentalist was next and the tabla player's fees finally depended on what the singer or instrumentalist decided to pay him. Even though my father was famous, he was paid 10 or 12 per cent of what the lead musicians earned.

NMK: Are we talking about 5,000 rupees a concert?

ZH: No! Are you kidding? In the 1960s, Abba may have been paid 500 or 1,000 rupees, while the lead musician was paid 15,000.

I remember once when Abba was on tour and the money that he used to send home had not come. Amma was down to her last five rupees and did not know if she could buy food for the next day, and so she went to sleep praying that some money would arrive.

That night she had a dream and Abba was in the dream. He gave her something wrapped in a handkerchief and when she unfolded it, there was a little bag with some money in it. The next morning, she said: 'Chal, Zakir' [Come, Zakir] and we headed towards Khar. We took a bus and got down opposite the Sacred Heart School on S.V. Road and made our way to the home of Rajendra Shankarji [Ravi Shankarji's brother] and his wife, Lakshmiji. When we arrived at their house, they welcomed us warmly. '*Aao, Bhabhi, kaisi ho? Sab theek hai?*' [Come, sister-in-law, how are you? All well?]

My mother was not the kind of person who could ask if her husband had sent anything for her—she was shy about such things—so she said nothing. Half an hour later, Lakshmi Shankarji said: 'Bhaiya has sent this for you.' And she handed Amma a handkerchief with a small bag wrapped in it. Some folded bank notes were in that bag.

Isn't that amazing?

NMK: Extraordinary! Your parents must have been deeply connected to each other.

ZH: They were. When Abba was home, they used to talk for hours at night. The story of her dream has stayed with me ever since.

NMK: Did those years of struggle influence your attitude towards money?

ZH: No. I was just grateful to do what I was doing. When I was thirteen or fourteen, I got to travel; nobody was watching over me, I did what I wanted, ate what I liked, and when we went on tour, I slept in a room of my own and didn't have to share it with four others. I had a radio and all that stuff. It was luxury. I got a lot of adulation too. I was as content as I am now. I was studying in an English-medium school and could read and write Urdu. I had memorized most of the Quran and am what they called at the madrasa, a hafiz. I was sometimes asked to read the Fatiha [the opening verse of a prayer] because I have a good memory.

NMK: Are you a religious person?

ZH: What is a religious person? I am a Muslim; my wife, Toni, is a Catholic; my daughters, Anisa and Isabella, were baptized; Taufiq's wife, Geetika Varde, is a Konkan Maharashtrian; Fazal's wife, Birwa, is a Gujarati from Ahmedabad—our family is a beautiful mix of universal oneness.

The fewer fences there are to climb, the better. I believe in the universality of humanity and that we are all one. None of the prophets, the Zoroastrians, Buddha, Mahavir or Guru Nanak have said anything different. They have all spoken of loving one another and striving for peace.

Being a musician has given me a how-to-be rulebook. The way I accompany the lead musician is the way I react to people in life. My solo performances are the way I hold court at a party, if I'm asked. Being a student, teacher, performer, composer—it's all of one piece. Ultimately everything for me revolves around music.

NMK: You said you had a good memory—for music you obviously do—but does that also apply to people and places?

ZH: I can recall a face almost in the place that I first saw it. I am a little hesitant in terms of names. But if someone tells me his or her name, I can remember what we talked about.

We meet so many people and you shake hands, etc., but I still remember people whom I am introduced to, because if you see them again you don't want to make them feel you've forgotten them. I think it's nice to remember names. When I am flying, I look at the badge of a stewardess, so that I can call her by her name, as opposed to saying: 'Excuse me, stewardess!' It establishes a different kind of interaction.

NMK: When you were telling me about the most unusual encounter your mother had with Gyani Baba around the time of your birth, I forgot to ask if you were born at home or in a hospital.

ZH: I was born on 9 March 1951 in a nursing home in Mahim at about 9:45 p.m. on a Friday. I don't remember the name of the nursing home, but I know it does not exist anymore. It was not far from our first place in Mahim. I used to pass it when I was a child, and someone pointed it out to me and said: 'That's where you were born.'

I came into this world after three girls—my elder sisters: Bilquis, Khurshid and Razia. There is a four-year gap between Khurshid Apa and me. I had a younger brother, Munawar, whom we called Munna, but we lost him when he was very young. Then came Fazal and Taufiq. There is a ten-year gap between Fazal and me, and an eleven-and-a-half-year gap between Taufiq and me. When we were growing up, I was more like an uncle to my brothers. Abba was travelling a lot, so I would often get them to practise the tabla. They told me that they were more scared of me than they were of Abba. [*smiles*]

I was very close to my sisters because we were about the same age. My elder sister Khurshid Apa is somewhat of a sentinel for our family. From the time that we were young, she has played the role of the eldest sibling and has continued to do so. She is concerned for each one of us. She keeps in touch with the extended family, sending wishes and gifts in time for all occasions. Caring for everyone's needs has made her the information-and-help junction. From time to time, she would even call Toni's mother in New York because that's a natural form of showing familial respect.

After her marriage to Ayub Bhai [Ayub Aulia], who is a published writer and poet, they settled in London. In Abba's name, her house is wide open to all visiting artists who are passing through London—they are invited for meals and given any help they need. She has kept in touch with the music community and kept us all connected. She has done all this while raising three children of her own: a daughter, Ghazal, and two sons, Ameer Najeeb and Mukarram Zaki.

Khurshid Apa is an Urdu poet and a writer. I still remember being so proud of her when her poem was published in the daily Urdu paper *Inquilab*.

After Abba's passing, she established the Alla Rakha Foundation and, in his name, has presented many young and deserving artists from India as well as those living in London. Khurshid Apa has kept the light on, and it is well known in the music community that her home is always open to them, in the same way that our home was a place of welcome for decades.

NMK: You said you lost a young brother.

ZH: The brother we lost was Munawar. He would have been a great musician. He could sing rhythms effortlessly when he was just a toddler. A rabid dog mauled him when he was three or four. They rushed him to the hospital and gave him every possible injection, but they could not save him. I was twelve years old at the time, and have always felt very guilty that I was not with him that day.

NMK: What a terrible trauma for the family.

ZH: It was. We also lost two sisters: the eldest, Bilquis Apa, passed away when she was very young. The family did not talk about it, but obviously it was painful. I don't know how she passed away. She died before I was born.

The second sister that we lost was Razia Apa. She was only fifty. That fatal day—2 February 2000—was a disastrous day for us. My brother Fazal and I were flying that morning to Kozhikode [Calicut] to play with Sultan Khansahib. We were at the Bombay airport and I just happened to call home and spoke to Razia Apa, who said she was going for her cataract surgery that morning. A year or two earlier my father had the same procedure at the same clinic and there had been no problem. It was a routine surgery; a piece of cake. Razia Apa said: 'I'll go today and get it done. Pray that it goes well.' I told Razia Apa to be careful, wished her luck, and asked her to keep me posted.

They were supposed to give her a local anaesthetic, so she had a little breakfast and went to the clinic on her own. Before the procedure could start, she apparently felt uneasy. The nurses did not know what was wrong with her, so they decided to postpone the surgery. After a short while, someone there suggested general anaesthesia, thinking it would be easier for Razia Apa. My sister probably agreed so that it would be over and done with.

Since she had eaten breakfast, they waited a while before the surgery, but not long enough. You're not supposed to eat before going under general anaesthetic. As you know, the muscles get paralysed, so during the operation, the food that she ate earlier entered her windpipe and she started to choke. They suddenly realized what was happening, but they did not have the right equipment or medication to revive her. When an ambulance finally arrived, she had already passed away.

By the time my younger brother Taufiq, who was at home in Bombay, managed to contact us in Kozhikode, we had already played the concert that evening and had just returned to the hotel. The news was utterly shocking. All I could tell Taufiq was to make sure that someone stayed close to our parents, to make sure they were being looked after. Some of Abba's students went immediately to Simla House, whilst Fazal and I desperately tried to find a way to get back to Bombay. We tried to hire a helicopter or charter a plane, but there was nothing we could do because the airport was closed for the night.

So Fazal, Sultan Khansahib and I drove from Kozhikode to Kochi. We got to Kochi around 4 a.m. on the morning of 3 February. When we got to the airport, we called home and were told that Abba had passed away. When he was told about Razia Apa, I believe he did not say a word. Though his students tried hard to distract him, he would not speak to anyone. Abba was very attached to Razia Apa. They were very close. I heard that Abba wandered around the house and even went into my room. Maybe he was thinking—where is Zakir? Perhaps he wanted to talk to me. But that didn't happen. He went to the bathroom and came out and that's when he had a heart attack. They called the doctor, but it was too late. When Fazal and I returned to Simla House, we arrived to two deaths in the family. I mean, how does this happen in any home? It doesn't really.

It was very strange. There were already forty guys from the press at our door. Word had spread, and it was difficult to manage everything. Amjad Ali Khansahib, Shivkumarji, Hariprasadji were there—everybody was there; I don't know how they heard the news. Amjad Ali Khansahib had come all the way from Delhi.

NMK: Was your father in good health otherwise? How old was he?

ZH: Abba was eighty. He was born in 1919 and he would have been eighty-one on 29 April 2000. He was in very good health. He passed away on a Thursday and on the previous Sunday he had played at Shanmukhananda Hall in Sion, in Bombay. He was fine. It was the shock of losing Razia Apa.

Amma was made of sturdier stuff and she oversaw all the arrangements. We had a family grave in the Mahim kabrastan and we had to find a second grave. They could not give us adjoining graves because there was no time. It was amazing to watch Amma get through everything. It required a lot of self-control and strength. The rest of the family sort of worked our way through the day as best as we could.

Abba passed away at around 3 a.m. on 3 February 2000, and by 7:30 or 8 that same morning, Fazal and I were home. Taufiq ran helter-skelter, making arrangements for the funeral. Abba and Razia Apa were buried on the same day and in the same graveyard in Mahim. Ravi Shankarji was in another city, so he chartered a plane and landed in time for the burial. He came straight to the graveyard.

I had even told Razia Apa to wait a day or two longer so that I could have gone with her to the clinic. But she said the procedure was routine and would take an hour, and it would be over. I heard that she felt uneasy that morning at the clinic, and perhaps if someone were with her she would've just returned home.

We decided not to take the doctors to task about Razia Apa. What would that have achieved? Then losing Abba on the same day…

NMK: The 'Homage to Abbaji' concerts have a huge following. The first concert starts at 6 a.m., the second around 2 p.m. and the last at 7.30 p.m. on the same day. A wide variety of musicians perform each year and it has become a big event for music lovers in Bombay. When did you first decide to organize these memorial concerts?

ZH: We did something on 29 April 2000, on Abba's birthday. I basically wanted to organize the barsi in the year that he had passed away, and only for that year. The morning concert was held out in the open at Kala Ghoda. We were allowed to block the surrounding area. That was probably the birth of the Kala Ghoda festival because it did not exist before that. We had this huge truck, which was turned into a stage. The afternoon session took place at the Tata Theatre. Without me even asking, musicians from all around the world came and, in the evening session, there were dozens of musicians and 8,000 of his fans who came to celebrate Abba's life.

In 2001, we decided to have the memorial concert on the day that Abba passed away [3 February]. 2016 is the sixteenth year since that first barsi. I don't even have to ask anyone, because so many musicians just say, 'I'll come.' I remember getting a text message from Amjad Ali Khansahib: '*Mian, hum haazir hain*' [I shall be there]. Abba had tremendous goodwill. Musicians just loved him. There was never any ill will against him, nor did anyone have a bad thing to say about him.

Every year on 1 February, we all visit the graves of Abba and Razia Apa. Then we go to Abba's music school and talk about him and remember him. The next day, we have a Quran khani [prayer meeting] at home and on 3 February, there's the barsi concert. It's a three-day process.

NMK: You were so close to your father. Does he appear in your dreams?

ZH: Every now and then he does. I am sure that some of the compositions that pop into my head when I'm sleeping are transmissions.

It is traditional for a father to recite prayers in the ear of a newborn, but Abba would hold me in his arms and sing rhythms to me. My mother used to scold him, and ask him to say a prayer instead, and Abba would tell her that music was his prayer. Sometimes I would be awake and sometimes not, but he carried on reciting rhythms to me during my infancy. I have this feeling those rhythms are somewhere in my subconscious and something triggers them and they come flooding back. Abba really believed that music is a divine language. He respected Goddess Saraswati as much as he believed in Islam.

NMK: Do you have premonitions or big dreams like your mother? I am thinking of her dream about your father sending her money when there was none at home.

ZH: No, no dreams like that. I probably dream more often about my mother than my father, because I spent more time with her. Till I was about twenty-two, and even when I came back and forth from America, my mother was always there. Abba was travelling so much.

Amma was the man of the house, for me. She was the one who made it possible that one day I could sit here trying to speak to you coherently about my life and my thoughts. I don't know why she felt that I must learn English. I don't know why she thought it was okay for a Muslim to go to a Catholic school. It must have been a difficult decision for her because her neighbours were like—why are you sending him there? He'll get corrupted—he'll become an angrez!

NMK: I am sure your mother visited you in America. Did she like it there?

ZH: She came to see us in 1983 but it took a while persuading her to come. She did not like flying and did not really enjoy America. She was a woman of the neighbourhood, a mohalla type of person. She liked standing on the balcony and chatting with the neighbours as they passed by: '*Arey Amina, kaisi ho, kya ho raha hai? Achchha Najma, kahaan ho? Namaz ho gayi?*' [Amina, how are you? What's going on? I say, Najma, where were you? Have you said your prayers?]

Amma had lots of friends, not just from the neighbourhood, but many wives of my father's students became close to her. Our house was a full house with Abba's students, countless guests and us kids. Amma never let anyone leave the house without eating. She was forever in the kitchen.

She used to love the ten-minute walk from Simla House to the bazaar, with its chain of lively conversations. She knew everyone and everyone knew her. For her, America was like—what is this? Nobody walks down the street. Why does everyone drive a car? You go to a shop and they don't know you. They just give you a what-do-you-want look.

*

NMK: We had to stop our last conversation as you were heading back to America. It's good to meet and talk again today. You've just arrived in Bombay, but you look surprisingly well rested. No jet lag?

ZH: I don't think so. I landed from the US the day before yesterday at four in the morning, came home, rested till nine, then gathered some clothes and the tabla, got into the car and drove to Pune. I arrived there at 2 p.m., had a little lunch, took a shower, ironed my kurta, got ready and was on stage by 6:45 in the evening. I played till about 10 p.m., then we went to the promoter's house for a nice dinner and I came back to my hotel at 1 a.m. I went to sleep till seven, had breakfast, got ready and then we drove to Baramati. Had a little something to eat at Baramati, warmed up the tabla, played the concert, had dinner, got into the car and drove for five-and-a-half hours back to Bombay. I got here at 4:30 this morning.

I don't feel that I'm being squeezed out of every ounce of energy. I feel fine today. And the glow is from interacting with the Pune audience, and the audience in a smallish city like Baramati. It's a tonic. There were kisans, people who work in cooperatives, some industrialists and many students.

There were about 1,500 people. We might have had a larger audience, but people did not have the cash to buy tickets, what with the recent demonetization in India. So only 1,500 people could come.

NMK: As far as performing in public goes, I read on the Net that you were five when you performed on the stage for the first time.

ZH: I don't remember it very clearly. Did I show you a photograph of me on stage? I looked more like seven or eight. It was one of those long, six-hour concerts, and I believe at some point my father may have needed to go to the loo or something, and so he asked me to take over because the concert was still in progress. That's how it happened. I just took over and started playing. I think the audience was a little dazed, but the maestro who was playing was totally okay.

NMK: The maestro?

ZH: Ali Akbar Khansahib.

NMK: Wow! What a way to start!

ZH: [*smiles*] My relationship with Khansahib goes back a long way. After this first time on the stage when I was seven or eight, I earned my first hundred rupees playing the tabla for him at the Bombay Press Club. That was when I was twelve. Then, from 1972, I spent about eleven years in America as his accompanist. I used to stay for six months or so in the US, and then come home for about four months, do concerts in India, and go back again.

Khansahib and I performed together all around the world and I taught at his music college. I mixed his drinks for him and sat with him through the evening. At some point, he would say: 'You eat, I'll eat later.' At around 2 a.m., he would have a piece of chicken and then go to bed. He ate very little and never drank before a concert. Khansahib just enjoyed a glass of whisky with three quarters' soda, after the sun had gone down.

NMK: Was it a big decision for him to move to America? Why did he decide to settle there?

ZH: I imagine it was not a very big decision. If he wanted to do something, he did it without thinking of the consequences.

Khansahib's first visit to America happened by accident. In 1955, Yehudi Menuhin, the great violinist, was organizing a series of Indian classical music concerts at New York's Modern Art Museum and he invited Ravi Shankarji to perform. As Raviji was busy at the time, he asked Yehudi Menuhin: 'Why don't you invite my brother-in-law, Ali Akbar Khan?' So that's how Khansahib was the first to visit America and not Ravi Shankarji.

Khansahib really enjoyed America during that first trip. Suddenly you were no longer a second-class citizen as you were in the India of the 1950s, and here you were counted amongst the music elite. You were wined and dined and given all that respect. Khansahib was the first Indian musician to perform on American television—in Alistair Cooke's famous arts programme *Omnibus*.

The following year, in 1956, Ravi Shankarji went to the States. Then, some years later, Khansahib was invited back to teach at the American Society for Eastern Arts in California. He jumped at the idea because he wanted to experience America again. So, he returned to Berkeley in 1965 to teach and in 1967, he founded the Ali Akbar College of Music, which soon moved to San Rafael in Marin County, and that's where his college is now.

I think living in America took him away from the rigmarole of daily life, the responsibility of being the prince of the house. He did not like all the attention he received in India—in California, he enjoyed vacuuming his house and watering his garden—he did this every day till he was no longer physically able.

NMK: Did you meet Ali Akbar Khan's father? The great Ustad Allauddin Khan.

ZH: I saw him once in Maihar. We went there to attend the celebration of Baba's hundredth birthday.

NMK: I read somewhere that he was very unpredictable and had a legendary bad temper. There is a 1971 documentary about Ravi Shankar called *Raga: A Journey to the Soul of India*, directed by Howard Worth, that I saw and, in the film, we see Ravi Shankar going to Maihar for Ustad Allauddin Khan's hundredth birthday. Is this the same trip that you're talking about?

ZH: That's right. I was about thirteen or fourteen and studying in the eighth standard. I travelled along with my father in the Kashi Express from Bombay to Maihar, which is in Madhya Pradesh. The train did not usually stop at Maihar, but at Katni and Satna. Because Ravi Shankarji was visiting Allauddin

Khansahib, and they were filming his visit, arrangements were for the Kashi Express to stop at Maihar, and so that's where we all got off. You will not see us in the Maihar portion of the film because it was really about Ravi Shankarji.

I remember that Allauddin Khansahib had gathered many of the local people and taught them how to play music. He created something called the Maihar Band. He would walk around with a stick and had the reputation of hitting these orchestra members if they made a mistake. He would get very angry.

Ali Akbar Khansahib used to say that, when he was young, his father would tie Khansahib's hair with a rope to a ceiling hook. And if he happened to fall asleep when practising and his head would droop, the rope would pull him up. There are many well-known stories about Baba being a hard taskmaster. I guess all teachers are. Maybe he became crankier in old age; sometimes the older you get, the crankier you can become. But come to think of it, I never saw Ali Akbar Khansahib in a cranky mood. He was as calm at eighty as he was at sixty.

NMK: Had his father passed away by the time he had moved to America?

ZH: No. But he did go back to his father's home in Maihar for a couple of months every winter, like I used to come to Bombay. Ali Akbar Khansahib's first wife and kids lived in Calcutta, and his second wife and kids lived in Bombay. His third wife was with him when he passed away. He had twelve children.

NMK: When you went to America for the first time, was it to work with Ali Akbar Khan?

ZH: No, Ravi Shankarji called me there. I was in Munich playing at a concert in February 1970 and Ravi Shankarji phoned me and said: 'Your father is unwell and can't do the four or five concerts that I have yet to do. Since you are in Germany, just go to the American Embassy, get a visa and meet me in New York.'

At that time, a young man of eighteen, who did not have dozens of documents, could walk into the American Embassy and apply for a visa. So I got my visa and left for America. I was Ravi Shankarji's tabla accompanist at the Fillmore on 22 February 1970 in San Francisco. After the short tour was over, I was about to return to India when Raviji heard about an opening in the Department of Ethnomusicology at the University of Washington in Seattle. It was he who advised me to stay on in America and take the teaching job. I taught and studied ethnomusicology. Because I was teaching, I did not have to pay university fees.

The plan was to get a PhD degree, but halfway through, I heard that Ali Akbar Khansahib's tabla player, Shankar Ghosh, had to return to India, and so Khansahib asked me to move to the Bay Area, to become his accompanist and teach at his music college in San Rafael. He understood that he needed a competent tabla player who was not a great master, but someone who could teach the students the basic blocks. I was young and not the Ustad Allarakha of my time, and all Khansahib needed was a simple tabla player to play a little rhythm for him on stage. Like Ravi Shankarji, he was aware that his concerts had to entertain the audience, and a musician with whom he could have a little *nok jhonk* [musical banter] was good. So I fit the bill.

I left Seattle and joined Khansahib in San Rafael, which is about 24 kilometres from San Francisco. I slept in his living room for the first ten days. It was just he and I and his cookbook! He was a good cook and made delicious biryani, daal and chicken curry. A few weeks later, he found me a rented room and, after that, I got my own apartment.

There was a huge and beautiful stained-glass mural of Goddess Saraswati that you'd see as you approached Khansahib's college. And inside his home, hung on his wall were symbols and images of every possible God and Goddess—Goddess Saraswati, Lords Ganesh and Krishna and Jesus—and Allah's name and the name of Prophet Muhammad were written in Arabic. Perhaps this came from his childhood in Maihar. The famous Ma Sharda Devi temple is located in his hometown. To reach the temple, which is on a very high hill, you have to climb more than a thousand steps. Inside the temple, images and symbols of every religion greet you. Perhaps those images stayed in Khansahib's mind.

He had a universal Sufi way of approaching his faith. Just think of the name of his sister—Annapurna Devi—that's not a Muslim name and, even though his family were Muslims, they were totally secular.

NMK: What did you learn from him on a personal level?

ZH: He was a quiet person. He would sit for hours and chain-smoke. If you asked him a question, he'd answer you, light up a cigarette and go quiet again. He was one of those people you could spend years with and suddenly realize that you had learned a lot without knowing it—both in terms of music and as a human being.

Ali Akbar Khansahib reminded me of a glass snow globe—the kind you shake and watch the snow whirling around inside. He had this calm exterior with a storm raging within. In many ways, he was a law unto himself; a man in his own world. He was like a sadhu who decides to stand on one leg for years on end. He did not conform, and everything rotated on an axis of his choice. It was amazing—he and his brother-in-law, Ravi Shankarji, were in America at the height of the popularity of Indian classical music, but Khansahib did not care to profit from it. He never attempted to find himself an agent to book concerts and earn him thousands of dollars. He liked going to his music school from 5 to 9 p.m., four days a week; he would teach there and then come home.

That's the kind of a person he was. But when it came to the administration of his own world, he was probably more frugal than my mother. [*both laugh*]

NMK: It sounds like he had no sense of envy.

ZH: No envy at all. Perhaps one of the things that I have learned from him is to be content and satisfied with whatever you create, and accept things the way they are. The other thing I learned from him was not to feel threatened. I can be competitive because I need to do things to express myself, but there was no need to feel threatened by the talent of others.

NMK: Ali Akbar Khan lived for many years in America. Do you feel he missed India?

ZH: I don't think he missed India, but he missed certain things. He would call me and say: '*Jhakir, kahin se shaami kebab le kar aao.*' [Jhakir, get me some shaami kebabs from somewhere.] He called me 'Jhakir', as he couldn't pronounce 'z' because he was a Bengali and there is no 'z' sound in Bengali.

Only once did I hear him speak of something he wanted very much. He wanted to meet the singer Noor Jehan! And as far as I know, Khansahib never got to meet her. Noor Jehan did not come to America, and in later years he stopped travelling. This was a regret of his—never meeting Noor Jehan.

He used to listen to her old songs, like *'Chanda re chanda'* from a 1972 Pakistani film called *Baharon Phool Barsao*. There was another song that went something like: *'Tere pyaar mein ruswa ho kar jaayen kahaan deewane log. Jaane kya kya pooch rahe hain ye jaane anjaane log.'* [Dishonoured in your love, where do I go? Wherever I go, I am asked about you.]

I used to argue with Khansahib and say that Mehdi Hassan Sahib sang this song first. He would immediately say: 'No, no, no! Noor Jehan sang it first.' 'But Mehdi Hassan Sahib has also sung it.' 'It was Noor Jehan.'

He liked her songs from *Anmol Ghadi* as well.

NMK: You mean the famous *'Awaaz de kahaan hai'* (Call out to me, where are you) from Mehboob Khan's *Anmol Ghadi*?

ZH: *'Awaaz de kahaan hai.'* Yes.

NMK: Those eleven years, between the ages of eighteen to twenty-nine, were spent in his company. It was undoubtedly an impressionable time in your life. Did Ali Akbar Khan become a kind of father figure for you?

ZH: He was not interested in becoming a father figure—that was the attractive thing about him. He did not behave like that even with his own sons. He had left India and so was not around his children who lived in Calcutta. His elder son Aashish knew him well, whilst the others were just teenagers.

I was a very young man, and he was about thirty years older, but he treated me as a colleague. How shall I put it? There was a compression of generations. He did not want to burden me or impose on me. Or make me deal with his great standing in music. The time that I spent with him was special—we played concerts and travelled to many cities. I taught at his music college and, when my class was over, I observed him teaching his students. He addressed everyone as 'aap'. He would say to me: *'Aap kahaan the? Aap ne khana khaya?'* [Where were you? Have you eaten?] He addressed everyone with great respect and made you feel that it was you who was on the higher pedestal.

NMK: A sign of a very confident and cultured person.

ZH: Yes—making you comfortable but at the same time ending up making you very uncomfortable. [*both laugh*]

One day he walked into my house with Mary Johnson, a young American who had first studied the tabla with Abba and then with me, and said: 'I have come to ask your permission.' I was flabbergasted: 'What, Khansahib?' He said calmly: 'We're getting married, and you are her teacher, so I have come to ask for your permission.' Now imagine that.

Mary became his third wife and it was she who was with him when he passed away in San Anselmo on 18 June 2009. He was eighty-seven. Mary Johnson Khan runs his college now. The then Indian prime minister, Manmohan Singh, wanted to bring his body back to Maihar and build a mausoleum in his name, but Khansahib's family knew that he would not have wanted that. He was happy in America. He liked the simplicity and normality of his life there. Having said that, when he played his sarod, it was never a normal event—he could move the heavens. It was a sublime experience, watching him.

I remember we were once playing in Patna. It was in October during Dussehra and it was very hot. Those big round white arch lights were directed on the stage, and it made us feel even hotter. Khansahib was almost completely bald and had a little hair on either side of his head. While he was playing, I noticed that his hair had started to grow. Suddenly there was this jet-black stuff on his head. I looked closely and what did I see? There were dozens of little insects and mosquitoes that had settled on his scalp and he was totally oblivious of them—he just went on playing. He was somewhere else.

NMK: Amazing. When Ali Akbar Khan passed away, in his obituary, Robert E. Thomason of the *Washington Post* (20 June 2009) included a fabulous quote by the master sarod player that I'd like to add here: 'If you practice for ten years, you may begin to please yourself, after twenty years you may become a performer and please the audience, after thirty years you may please even your guru, but you must practice many more years before you finally become a true artist—then you may please even God.'

ZH: It speaks of Khansahib's depth of awe towards this tradition.

In some ways, it leads the followers to believe it is hopeless. [*laughs quietly*] Here's this person who is talking about fifty years and, at the end, you may even please God. At the same time, Khansahib himself was a professional musician at eighteen. But maybe he was talking about the kind of maturity you achieve over the years as your understanding of music grows, and your knowledge is more complete.

His statement leaves you wondering, but does not tell you something definite. 'You *may* even please God,' it is not you *will* please God. This quote is one of those gems that could hint at where we need to arrive. It is also saying that even if you do arrive, you are not there yet. It's true that perfection may not exist, but what are you saying? 'Don't do music. It's an uphill struggle and when you do get all the way up, a bear will eat you.' [*both laugh*]

Ali Akbar Khansahib was a great teacher. But many old maestros did paint a picture of this art form in terms like: 'Yes, you should do it, but it's unattainable.' Was that a good way to go about it? I don't know. You need to speak of the importance of music, to tell students what an awe-inspiring tradition it is, but do you use such superlatives that make it an impossible task? Is this testing the will of the student, or trying to tell the student to go away?

If you are a teacher, you have a certain responsibility towards your students and so you tell them this is the kind of path you must follow, because this is going to get you near to where you need to be. That's a positive approach. If you tell them it's unattainable, you put cement on their feet and say I am going to drop you in the water and you're going to sink, even if you try to swim.

My father never did that. He never gave me the impression that it was an impossible mountain to climb. He used to say:

'Try this, do this, do that. What I see when I look at this mountain is not what you will see when you look at it. The peak may appear in a different place to me, but that's ok. One step at a time and just go through this process.'

NMK: I was watching a beautiful interview with Ali Akbar Khan on his website, in which he said he never saw his father's eyes because his own eyes were always lowered in Baba's company. I found that so moving.

In view of the kind of taskmaster his father was, perhaps Ali Akbar Khan's quote makes sense when he says he might never attain his goal.

ZH: Yet, the simplicity of the man was in wanting to meet Noor Jehan! So, which was the true him?

You have to realise that most of the things that ended up as quotes by Khansahib were spoken in the company of American students and followers. They looked at him with awe, and I understand that he felt the need to tell them how special and sacred this music was, but in doing so, did the description end up assuming inhuman proportions?

Believe me, if I had read that quote twenty years ago, I would have nodded my head in agreement and said: 'Yeah, yeah.' But my thinking over the years, I hope, has become more rational, more realistic. I think about how this art should be transmitted, as opposed to seeing it as a mythological impossibility.

I must tell you, Khansahib was a man who rarely practised. A trait that we all appreciated was when he was performing on stage he never felt the need to please the audience. The entire musical fraternity around the world, including me, regard him as a musical genius, and I have noticed this about musical geniuses, including Khansahib—that one day his performance was a sublime experience that would get you talking for the next twenty years, and on another day it was a more ordinary experience. This was simply because he was not worried about tripping and falling on his face. How did that matter?

I am fortunate that I happened to be in the right place at the right time and that he asked me to work with him. He could have called a tabla player from Calcutta—maybe it was just a coincidence that he asked me—but, in any case, I would have happily given my right leg, not my hand, to work with him!

I met my wife Toni in Khansahib's Fairfax house.

NMK: Was your wife, Antonia Minnecola, a student at his college?

ZH: Not when we first met.

We're talking about the time when the American music world was going through a 'discover India phase'. Toni's best friend Judy [Lynn McDowell] was working with Michael Butler, the producer of the rock musical *Hair*, and they were considering producing a musical with an Indian theme. So, Judy had gone to meet Ali Akbar Khansahib and the college director Jim Kohn, to discuss the possibility of collaborating on the musical.

Later in the summer, Judy invited Toni to come to LA, where a student from Ali Akbar College, who was writing songs for the musical, suggested they all go together to the college, since the autumn session was about to begin. Toni attended a concert at the college and sat in on some classes.

Judy was going to meet Khansahib again, so Toni accompanied her to Khansahib's home, with the intention of asking him whether she could join the college. Toni had been attending a few classes at the Manhattan School of Music, right before coming to California. I happened to be at Khansahib's house that evening and that's where we met. I think it was sometime in late September of 1971.

Khansahib's son Aashish and I had a sort of fusion band and Toni came to hear us play at a club that same night. Khansahib had given her permission to study at the college, so she stayed on and Judy left. Toni began studying Kathak and the required vocal, taal and theory classes, and over the following months we kept running into each other. Eventually I asked her out.

I could not afford to take her to a nice restaurant, so we went to Jack in the Box and then to Sausalito, which is about an eight-mile drive from San Rafael. We had ice cream there, watched the full moon and walked along the bay. It was a very special evening, filled with a sense that something great was making its way into our lives.

We became an item, but were not fully committed to each other. We lived together in different places and, finally, in 1976, we found a place where we could stay more permanently and it was there that we had our nikah.

NMK: So you got married in the States?

ZH: We had three marriage ceremonies in the US. The first was a civil marriage on 22 August 1978, then a church wedding on 23 September, which Toni wanted, and on 11 November we had a nikah ceremony, which Abba and Amma wanted.

Toni's mother did not come to California for the nikah because it was too soon after the church wedding, and so Ravi Shankarji gave Toni away. Toni's father had passed away many years earlier. My father was there and Ali Akbar Khansahib was a witness, so this very interesting little wedding took place in San Anselmo.

NMK: When did your parents first meet her?

ZH: Abba met Toni around the time we were living together. She went to New York in the summer of 1976 to study with him and to look after him. They knew each other from that time, and things were fine. My mother first met Toni when she came to India to further her dance studies in the winter of 1974-75.

NMK: Do you think your parents would have preferred that you had married an Indian?

ZH: As you can imagine, they thought I could have the pick of the crop. There was a guy who owned beedi factories in Bangalore and who wanted me to marry both his daughters because the sisters did not want to be separated! My parents imagined Zakir inheriting a beedi factory. [*laughs*] There were stories like that about possible brides, but somehow Abba was convinced that my marrying Toni would not come in the way of my music.

We were very young when we got married. I was about twenty-seven. Toni had just come to know Indian music, and I had just come to know the West, so we helped each other understand the other's world. Through her, I could understand what America was all about. Toni continues to be a sounding board for me, like Amma was for Abba. My way of thinking has a lot to do with our conversations over the years. She knows how to support me with the right amount of smiles, and the right amount of seriousness. She encourages me to take bold decisions and has shown even greater recklessness than me in abandoning everything to pursue music. She was instrumental in my getting involved with all kinds of music. 'Play music with this guy, work with him; you must hear him, you must hear her.' My work with Charles Lloyd, Edgar Meyer, Béla Fleck, or Alonzo King LINES Ballet is all her initiative.

Toni was very involved in Indian dance and studied Kathak with Sitara Deviji for nearly thirty years, until Sitaraji's death in November 2014. My wife was a very devoted student. And instead of making a name for herself, she devoted herself to our daughters and to me.

NMK: So Toni holds the fort?

ZH: She always has. It was her energy that allowed us to set up our record company, Moment Records, in 1991. She co-produces the albums with me and, as the art director, she writes and edits the liner notes and the artists' bios, besides overseeing the business side of things. I have no clue how to pay taxes or bills.

Toni co-produced all my American and European tours from 1986 to 2008, until I started working with IMG Artists Ltd. Toni is dedicated to bringing the right focus to my music, and to Indian classical music. She's my best friend, best critic and best support.

NMK: Was her family happy to accept you?

ZH: They were fine. I had spent so much time in America so it was easier for them. There was no language issue. It was initially very difficult for Amma—the first hurdle was the language—she could not communicate in English. So, that was difficult, but my wife learned a little Hindi. Amma eventually realized that Toni was the best person for me, and she was in fact more Indian than an Indian wife my mother might have found.

You know, my work takes me away from home a lot. And that's not always easy. In my struggling days, I would go to Europe for a concert tour with Hariprasad Chaurasiaji and, once that was over, there would be an eight or ten-day gap before Shivkumarji's tour would begin. I could not afford to go back to the US for ten days, because it was more economical for me to stay with my sister Khurshid Apa in London. Biding my time in London meant being away from home for a longer period, and that was very difficult for the family. I remember when Toni was pregnant with our elder daughter, Anisa, I went to India for the concert season and then to Europe with Shivji and Hariji, and when I came back, Toni was very pregnant. That's how much time had passed. A similar thing happened when our second daughter, Isabella, was born.

NMK: You're mobbed after every concert, and if you are spotted in a public space, people instantly crowd around you. How do you deal with your stardom?

ZH: Stardom? That's not my problem. That's an image others have created. Down the line, it will be over, so why worry about it? I don't want to be caught up in a world that's a passing breeze. I often quote the kahawat [adage] 'Every dog has his day'. Perhaps I am the dog today. I could get used to the adulation and love, but five years down the road, I won't have it. So, I am going to have to get unused to adulation.

Sometimes Toni and I giggle about the attention I get. She knows that I don't really care about it and she is not the type to let it affect her either. I remember we were once at a dinner in Venice, where Sophia Loren was a guest. My wife loves this fine Italian actress, but it would not occur to her to cross the room and shake hands or take a picture with the star. She was just happy being in Sophia Loren's proximity.

NMK: How do you react to fans and the selfie mania?

ZH: It happens all the time. I don't mind it. This morning at the airport, the guys who look after the trolleys, the security guys, and the customs officers all wanted pictures with me. And I obliged. There were some passengers who wanted selfies too. I was on the train heading to my terminal at the Dubai airport, and the train passengers wanted photos. It's okay.

NMK: Have you wanted to take a selfie with anyone?

ZH: Oh God! Maybe some fellow musicians, and of course my granddaughter. I've done selfies with her. For instance, I was performing at a concert yesterday with Shankar Mahadevan and Louiz Banks, and they were taking photos and stuff. My cellphone was off and in my bag. [*laughs*]

NMK: I believe you were voted the sexiest man in India by the female readers of an Indian magazine called *Gentleman* in 1994.

ZH: I thought that was very funny. The magazine team came to see me and wanted me to wear all these suits and jackets and Western clothes, and feature on their cover. I think they were equally shocked and surprised that I won the greatest number of votes because they had assumed the winner would be Amitabh Bachchan. I think the result must have been a downer for them, because they weren't going to get the kind of publicity they wanted from the poll result. [*both laugh*]

NMK: You've lived in America for decades now, and currently there is a growing anti-Muslim feeling there. Did you sense a change in attitude towards you?

ZH: I give credit to the vast majority of Americans whose thinking, I hope, has not been altered by what's happening in the US now. That's the way I see it.

I work in a world dominated by musicians and creative artists who don't think twice about who prays in a church, mosque or temple. That has never been the issue. The same applies to artists in India.

We are going through a very tense time in America. But, generally speaking, when you live, like we do, in a place like California, you live among a diverse population, and I believe this makes for a more progressive and tolerant society.

Coming back to your question, I don't feel personally discriminated against as a Muslim in America or in India, or anywhere else in the world. Is this a defence mechanism? I don't know, but I have never felt under scrutiny. The kind of environment I inhabit is sympathetic to the person that I am and is totally supportive of what I do.

You know, in the summer of 2016, I got a call from the White House, wanting to give me the President's Medal of the Arts. There was a new rule that non-Americans could not receive the medal, but I was nevertheless nominated.

NMK: Talking about awards, I hear the San Francisco Jazz Center gave you a Lifetime Achievement Award on 18 January 2017. How was the event for you?

ZH: My God, it was fantastic! It was more than I could have ever imagined. There were four days of celebrations and an incredible gala. The dining room was full and every chair was taken. There were about 900 invitees. There were speeches by Nancy Pelosi and the mayor, and many community leaders.

And then, surprise-surprise—my daughter Anisa made a five-minute film on me that was shown there, and in which many great musicians commented on my music. I didn't know she was making the film and it was like, wow! In her film, many musicians, including Herbie Hancock, Vijay Iyer, Eric Harland, the music director of the San Francisco Symphony Michael Tilson Thomas—each a master—talked about me. Other great musicians like Joe Lovano, during his musical offering, made generous comments. It was so moving. Anisa had also interviewed Charles Lloyd, who spoke about a concert at Grace Cathedral in San Francisco where we had played together and which was billed 'The Sacred Space'. This was just after 9/11 and the promoters were scared that people would not come to the concert for fear of crossing the Golden Gate Bridge, thinking that somebody was going to blow it up. Charles Lloyd said: 'I was talking to Zakir about it, and Zakir very quietly said: "Music should be used for building bridges not destroying them."' Listening to Charles Lloyd, I realized that we are all learning from one another. Even though they are masters, they are also looking for knowledge and validity and recognition of being on the right track.

When I thanked everyone at the event, I said I had been given a pat on my back, but it did not mean I had arrived at the end of my journey. I have to take the next step. I suddenly remembered the Robert Frost line 'Miles to go before I sleep'.

The whole event was very loving and emotionally charged. And after the film's screening, my dear friend Mickey Hart presented the award to me and made a speech. It felt very surreal, and I was not sure whether I was awake or asleep, or in a Fellini movie! It was quite an experience. It reminded me of being in a room in our Mahim house, playing the tabla and peeping through the open door to see whether Abba was watching. And if he were watching, would he react and say something like: 'Do this, or do that?' A reaction from him was in some way a confirmation that I had got through to him and he liked what I was playing. That's how I felt during the event. All these people were talking and I was in this room, doing all these things, and hoping that these great masters would accept what I had done and show me what to do next.

NMK: This must not have been the first lifetime achievement award that you received?

ZH: It was the first that came from that world. My main act is traditional Indian music and there is this cousin form, jazz. It is a whole world in itself; it has a life and tradition. A different protocol governs it. For them to accept this guy from another part of the world and embrace him as one of their own, is a landmark moment—that Indian music and jazz have some distant relationship and it is not necessary to be apart—and instead to cross that bridge.

NMK: Were you the first Indian to receive this award?

ZH: Yes. But it's just a pat on the back. To me it meant that I am on the right path and the place where I'm heading is where I should be going.

NMK: I browsed the SF Jazz Center website, where the gala in your name was widely publicized. I'd like to add a quote by Herbie Hancock that appears on their website: 'Everybody wants to play with Zakir Hussain. He's amazing. He is able to transcend cultures and national borders.'

And you certainly have done that, and along the way you must have met and worked with many world musicians. Is there an encounter that left a deep impact on your playing?

ZH: For me the idea of rhythm as a multilayered entity was not very clear. I did not think of the tabla as providing a multi-sonic experience and I was just very happy to take the information given to me and whip it out on the instrument and have people applaud.

When I started playing concerts, the idea of exploring the instrument—of discovering various parts of the skin of the tabla, the right corner, the left corner, the centre, using the middle finger, the pinkie, the thumb, or just the palm, discovering how the tones change; and what kind of harmonics they suggest—all that was not part of my performance until I got talking to an extraordinary Latin jazz percussionist of

Afro-Cuban tradition called Armando Peraza. I met him when our band Shakti was touring with another group, led by a guitar player named Carlos Santana.

NMK: You say these names so casually! Santana, wow! [*both smile*]

ZH: Well! We were travelling together and performing every night. This was around 1975-76. We [Shakti] used to open the show—the guitar player John McLaughlin, the violinist L. Shankar, the ghatam maestro T.H. Vinayakram and myself—and Carlos Santana and his band took over, after us. At the end of the show, the drummers from both bands got together for a jam session on stage. Drummers can easily jam because rhythm is universal. After the concert, we would all go and have dinner somewhere or have a glass of wine.

During the first two or three shows, I noticed that Armando played his solo with five conga drums in front of him. The biggest one is called the tumba. When he played with Carlos Santana, he just provided the rhythm. But here it seemed to me that he was playing a song on his drums. You could hear different tones, you could hear melody; the kind of melody that you hear a guitar produce—there were so many melodic structures happening. And if you looked around the stage, there was just this one guy playing. I was very intrigued—this was amazing. I could see he was not treating the drums as only a rhythm voice, but he was coaxing as many sounds out of them as he could—exploring, cajoling, squeezing. 'If I play you here, come out and let me hear your reaction.' Listening to him was like a symphonic experience in rhythm.

Later, when I spoke to Armando, I said with great enthusiasm: 'Wow! You play all those rhythms and a melody on your drums.' He said: 'Melody? I am not playing a melody. No, I'm just talking.' Then he hummed a rhythmic sound, added some Spanish words, then some words in an African language, and finally he moved it all around to English. Suddenly it was a song. It all made sense to me—and it sparked this whole new idea in my head, to take my tabla, which had all those inherent possibilities, and somehow extract that kind of information and perform it for the audience. It was an incredible revelation.

The basic process started back then. It took me a while to figure it all out, but that's what I do now. In those days, you did not do that on the tabla. Because the tabla has tones, at times it can sound like some melodic stuff is happening—you can converse with a vocalist, or players of the flute, sitar and sarod—not just rhythmically but also melodically. But this was not part of our job description. As a tabla player, the job was to play and let the lead musician do whatever he was doing. When he looked at you and his eyes said: 'Okay, play a little,' you played and then pulled back.

I revelled in the fact that I had found something very special. Armando Peraza made me understand the harmonic and melodic ability of the tabla. He planted that seed. Isn't it strange how you have a tradition ten thousand miles away and it somehow fits like a glove with a tradition that belongs to another part of the world?

NMK: Many people talk about Indian music's influence on jazz, but it sounds like it works both ways. As you say, it's a cousin form.

ZH: Yes. It was after talking to Armando that I realized that Raviji and my father were doing more or less the same thing. Raviji had found a way to turn Indian music into an entertaining art form. He lit that fire. On stage, you could see his ability to charm. When he and Abba played together, they conversed with each other like two jazz musicians. In earlier times, this was not something that Indian music was about. It was about the main guy and everyone else just following.

NMK: I saw your father and Pandit Ravi Shankar playing in Paris in the 1970s. Concerts themselves have this strong visual element, and, that evening, I remember we the audience took so much from their physical presence—the way they commanded the stage, the way they sat, the way they held their instruments, the way they smiled at each other. They were conversing just as you've described. A great sense of complicity was established between performer and audience.

ZH: Had you seen Ustad Vilayat Khansahib or other great sitarists on stage, you would not have found that kind of interaction. They were unaware that musical conversations would appeal to the audience. But Ravi Shankarji understood that.

I think the way Indian musicians communicate on stage with one another today has a lot to do with Ravi Shankarji and Abba starting those musical conversations back then.

NMK: We have spoken about your playing tabla with numerous instrumentalists. I am sure you have accompanied many vocalists too. Am I right?

ZH: Well, this is the bane of tabla players who become a little well known; we are rarely booked to play with vocalists.

In earlier times, I've played the tabla for many singers, including Nirmala Deviji, Shobha Gurtuji, Kishori Amonkarji, Ghulam Mustafa Khansahib, Bhimsenji and Pandit Jasrajji. As a twelve-year-old, I played with Pandit Omkarnath Thakurji.

I used to go to Walkeshwar every Sunday to Bade Ghulam Ali Khansahib's house and be available to play rhythm for him. Khansahib's wife considered my mother as her daughter. So they thought of me as a grandson, and the order conveyed to my parents was to send the grandson over on Sundays. My father understood the importance of it and said I should go. I was not hired to play tabla for Khansahib, he just wanted me around to soak in whatever was going on. Sometimes he would have visitors over, and, at other times, he would just sit talking to his wife or to his younger son, Munawar Ali Khansahib. If the mood was upon him, he would start singing, and then my job was to play the tabla. The whole idea was that I should understand that world and learn what I needed to know about vocal music; to get the tools that I would need in the future.

When I went to Calcutta for the first time, I was instructed to go to his house, before being taken to where my father was staying. A Mr Das picked me up from Howrah Junction Railway Station and took me straight to Park Circus, where Bade Ghulam Ali Khansahib was living. I paid my respects, and he talked to me for a few moments. Of course, his wife, whom I called Bari Amma, gave me a big hug and something to eat, and then I was sent on my way to Abba.

Khansahib lived in Calcutta before moving to Bombay. Calcutta was a great centre for music and arts in those days and was home to many musicians. Sometimes Abba too would stay there for five weeks at a time, playing concerts all around the area: in Malda, Sealdah, Bardhaman and Kharagpur. Concerts would be held in Calcutta itself. There was the Park Circus Conference, Dover Lane Music Conference, All Bengal Conference and Uttarpara Conference.

Once, when Bade Ghulam Ali Khansahib was visiting Bombay, the great singer Ganga Bai convinced him to move here. She was living near Opera House and helped Khansahib to get a place in Walkeshwar.

NMK: What kind of person was he?

ZH: He was totally immersed in music. He appeared to be in a cocoon of sonic beauty. To see an artist so involved in his expressive mode is something. Time had no meaning for him. If you wanted to be a part of his music, you sat there and took what was coming at you. The expression and emotionality of his singing triggered a reaction in the people around him. That was probably when I first learned about the rasa element in music—to hear how love, longing, sadness, melancholy and devotion are expressed.

Just as Abba had been sent to Ashiq Ali Khansahib to understand how the emotional content is expressed through the voice, that's what I was learning in the presence of Bade Ghulam Ali Khansahib. I think it helped me to become a more expressive tabla player. It may not have helped me at that point in time, but later I could use it and decipher it in my own way. You know how it is; you hear something and only later do you realize what it really is. I found accompanying a vocalist very stimulating and challenging.

I have also had the honour of playing the tabla for other wonderful singers, including Girija Deviji, Nisar Hussain Khansahib, the great Sahaswan-gharana singer. And in the 1980s, I organized some tours for Pandit Jasrajji in America and travelled with him. We have played together in Bombay and Pune, and in other cities as well.

NMK: Why is a vocalist more effective than an instrumentalist in expressing emotions?

ZH: Because he or she is singing words, and words add weight to the emotional experience, even though the lyrics are minimal in classical singing. I'll give you an example: 'Nahin aaye sawariya ghir aaye badariya' [Though my beloved has not come, the dark clouds are here]. Those few words let you understand and feel the melancholy, the sadness and the longing. The singer may sing that one line for twenty minutes, but in those twenty minutes the singer has fifty different ways of expressing complex emotions, and fifty different ways of subtly adjusting rhythm. As an accompanist, you can help the vocalist lift the performance to another plane for the audience.

NMK: Your analysis is so clear.

ZH: It's not an Archimedes-type discovery. It's just very logical. That's why most tabla players have to learn compositions that are sung, to understand the rasas at play, depending of course on the composition.

NMK: Sorry if I sound naive, but does an instrumentalist always aim to emulate the human voice?

ZH: We are told that the original music is vocal music and musical instruments were made to accompany vocal music or emulate it, and that's what instrumentalists try to do.

The intricate possibilities, however, of the voice that a very special singer can produce, the combinations or permutations of notes, are difficult to replicate on the sitar or sarod. The sitar has an easier time playing certain things, but the sarod does not, and that's why it's very difficult for some sarod players to transpose some of the sitar elements on to their instrument.

That's why Vilayat Khansahib and Ali Akbar Khansahib were unique instrumentalists because they came the closest to emulating vocal music. I must also add that they spent much time with vocalists. Vilayat Khansahib hung out with Amir Khansahib and when Ali Akbar Khansahib was a court musician in Jodhpur, he spent time with all the baijis—Gauhar Jaan, Siddheshwari Devi and Akhtari Bai, and also Faiyaz Khansahib—all those great singers.

I remember Ali Akbar Khansahib saying that he had accompanied Faiyaz Khansahib. And so had found a way of transposing those voice qualities on to the sarod, which is even more difficult than doing it on the sitar. Because the sitar has frets, you know where the notes are. But the sarod has no frets, so you're guessing where a particular note is. Despite that, Khansahib was able to transpose the human voice on to the sarod—no sarod player before him had ever done that. And the same goes for Vilayat Khansahib. No sitar player came close to emulating the human voice on the sitar in the way he did—the taans and murkis and khatkas and so on. Sometimes he would sing a melodic combination and then execute it on the sitar. You could hear it; it was right there. That is why Vilayat Khansahib is credited with having created the 'gayaki ang' style [suggestive of the human voice] for the sitar.

NMK: What skills do you need when playing tabla to match the footwork of, say, a Kathak dancer?

ZH: It's a unique and exciting challenge for any tabla player—it's a give-and-take situation. Unlike instrumental and vocal accompaniment, here the tabla player plays a dual role—that of a soloist and a lead voice of the nritta, pure dance, and at the same time is a support to the storytelling sections of the Kathak dancer's performance. To be a good accompanist, a tabla player must have a working knowledge of the repertoire and the ability to instantly transpose and execute the dance language on the tabla.

I was fortunate that in my teens I had played tabla for Kathak dancers in Bibi Bai Almas's home—we talked about this. I also spent time in the company of the great Sitara Deviji and her brother Chaube Maharajji. Much of my knowledge of dance comes from these two stalwarts. I was twelve years old when I performed for Sitara Deviji for the first time, and it was through her that I had the opportunity of playing for Birju Maharajji.

A festival of music and dance called Sur Singar Samsad was held in Bombay, and Birju Maharajji was to dance there with Pandit Samta Prasadji as his accompanist. As it turned out, Samta Prasadji's flight was cancelled. Hence he could not make it to the show. So Maharajji called Sitaraji to suggest a tabla player, and she decided to take me along. We went to Birla Hall and she introduced me to Maharajji. I was about fourteen or fifteen at that time and I must say that Birju Maharajji did not even ask her why she had brought a schoolboy to play tabla for him. He trusted her and gave me his blessings. Perhaps it was because my father had accompanied him when Birju Maharajji danced on my fourth birthday. That may have had something to do with his accepting me.

I must have done all right because on another occasion soon after that, Maharajji had me accompany him in Patna. I played quite often for him. He is a very fine tabla player himself and understands how to bring the best out of his tabla accompanists. I learned how to accompany stories from Birju Maharajji and from Sitaraji. Just as the dancer plays all the characters in a story, the tabla player portrays all the characters through his instrument, sonically amplifying the expressive and emotional aspects of dance.

Sitaraji was a great storyteller, a kathakar, and it was a pleasure to watch her and accompany her through the telling of these stories. With Maharajji it was different; it was the joy of spontaneously trading rhythm patterns, and together arriving at the 'sum' (first beat of the cycle) with no prior knowledge of how we would traverse this tricky highway of taal. It was, and is, very intoxicating.

My association with Maharajji and Sitaraji lasted forty years and I consider myself fortunate to have had them among my many mentors, and it is with deep gratitude that I acknowledge their guiding hand in my growth as a dance accompanist. I mentioned to you that Sitaraji just recently left us in November 2014. These were cherished and enlightened encounters.

NMK: How wonderful to be in a position where your understanding of music can come from so many sources. I am no expert in music but, like many non-experts, I too can feel the effect it has on emotions. I am wondering if you have been moved to tears on hearing a particular piece of music.

ZH: It doesn't necessarily have to be classical music. I've heard folk music that has moved me to tears.

We were judging a *Saregama* TV talent show, and Sonu Nigam was the anchor. That was the time when the judges were the decision makers and there was no voting through cell phones. We were filming this particular show in a New York studio and there was this singer from the Punjab province of Pakistan, and he sang this beautiful folk song. The song was all about the longing for home. It was so moving and so beautiful that I had tears in my eyes. I had forgotten that I was in front of the camera. I was a young man and I suddenly missed home. It was embarrassing but it happened. He sang so beautifully. So, it wasn't Bade Ghulam Ali Khansahib's thumri, '*Ka karun sajni aaye na balaam*', Ali Akbar Khansahib's Raga Chandranandan, Ravi Shankarji's Hameer, or Vilayat Khansahib's Bageshree that ended up moving me to tears.

*

NMK: We haven't met for a while and you've been so busy in the past few days. Zakir, thanks for making time for our book.

Can we start today by talking about musical instruments? How long does it take to get accustomed to, say, a new tabla?

ZH: In the world of music, and especially when it comes to traditional music, haste is not a good idea. You need time to build a relationship with your instrument. The instrument's spirit has to react and then things happen. You don't just buy a new sitar today, get on to the stage tomorrow and start playing it. The sitar must come into its own. You have to play it for some months before you feel comfortable—okay, now I can play it on stage.

What do I bring to the tabla? I think it is openness and clarity, and that is what we bring to the audience. What I present must make sense, whether that involves a heart-to-heart interaction between musical instrument and musician, or zero hesitancy in the thought process, or not worrying about the parameters—your musical statement must be created with as much clarity as possible.

I am reminded of a lovely incident. Kishan Maharajji was about to go on stage, when someone said: 'Maharajji, have a great concert.' He replied: '*Dekhenge bhaiya, aaj tabla kya kehta hai*' [Let's see, brother, what the tabla wants to say today].

It's the same with all instruments—the guitar, piano, bass, or violin. You need to have a relationship with the instrument, because you want it to do your bidding. It has to accept you, and show you that it is ready to take that leap of faith with you.

For example, I need the tabla skin to have a certain amount of give—so when I hit it, it must respond and resonate in a certain way. The tone should have a certain amount of bass, treble and mid-range. The pressure of my hand is different from the pressure of someone else's hand, therefore that impacts the thickness of the skin—how much extra skin must there be, so that it can bend in the way I want it to.

NMK: For those who don't already know, the word 'tabla' comes from the Arabic 'tabl' which means drum, but there are, in fact, two tabla drums—the smaller one is made of wood and called the dayan (the right drum) and the larger, deeper-pitched drum is made of metal and called the bayan (the left drum).

Making the tabla must be a very skilled job. Are tabla makers greatly appreciated?

ZH: I personally feel tabla makers in India don't get their proper due, nor do they get the kind of monetary return they should. If somebody in America makes a guitar by hand for a famous guitar player, they charge between $12,000 and $20,000. Béla Fleck is a master of the banjo, and some of his banjos are worth $120,000. All musical instrument makers in India are not really compensated enough or given the kind of respect and status they deserve.

In my case, Haridas Vhatkar has been making my instruments and repairing them for the past eighteen years. He used to live in Miraj, near Kolhapur, and as a young man he came to Bombay because he heard me play. He decided to learn how to make the tabla, so he could make them for me. Sometimes the parts are made in machines and then assembled together by someone who has the ear and knowledge, while Haridasji does everything from scratch—he gets the buffalo hide straps, polishes and cleans the goat skin to get the rough edges out, etc. It's all done by hand. The whole process can take weeks. The buffalo straps have to be soaked in oil to make them soft enough so that they can be pushed through the little grooves on the edges of the tabla and then tightened. All tabla makers sit on the floor and work—so all this pulling makes their backs go and it is murder on the hands. You can of course buy a standard tabla, which will not have even 10 per cent of the quality of Haridasji's work. He has become the Steinway of the tabla!

I have put Haridasji on a stipend. So, if I'm gone for eight months, he does not have to worry, he will still have some money coming in. He came to America in July 2016, during my retreat, and repaired the tabla for forty of my students. He made a bundle and came back to India. [*laughs*]

NMK: Good for him! When I think about the different Indian instruments, the sitar sounds less melodic than the flute or the violin to me. Sorry if it's stating the obvious.

ZH: One of the reasons why the sitar may not feel as melodious to you is because the flute is an out-and-out melodic instrument, and the violin is similar, whilst the sitar is both melodic and percussive. Because it has this rhythmic ability, the sitar can very easily feel overbearing. When Ravi Shankarji played, there was great emphasis on rhythm, but that's not what I noticed in Vilayat Khansahib's playing. He was more into exploring the sitar's melodic element. The rhythmic element came into his playing, but did not appear to dominate.

In the old days, there were no microphones and the instruments were not as finely made, so their resonance was very limited, therefore a more rhythmic style was played on the sitar. Listen to the old recordings, you'll find the sitar playing was somewhat based on the way the Afghani rabab is played.

In instrumental music, one style or school is called 'rababi' and the other is 'beenkaar'. The 'been' is an ancient instrument from which the surbahar and the sitar were created. The rabab is a lute-like instrument, more prominent in Afghanistan, and from there came this style of rhythmic playing. If you Google a rabab recording, you'll hear how rhythmic it is. They say that the sarod emerged from the rabab, but I'm not sure. I can't trace that lineage, but a lot of the rababis eventually became sarod players, like Amjad Ali Khansahib, his father Hafiz Ali Khansahib, and Hafiz Ali Khansahib's guru. On the other hand, Vilayat Khansahib and Ustad Allauddin Khansahib were from the beenkaar gharana.

It's strange, but when I was a young tabla player and I heard Ravi Shankarji and Ali Akbar Khansahib play a duet, the sitar sounded very pleasant to me and the sarod sounded very aggressive. I don't know why. Later, when I started accompanying Khansahib and got to hear the sarod a lot more, the depth of that instrument emerged and I realized it had a much better balance of melody and rhythm. I became a fan of the sarod, but that happened only when I was about twenty-one years old. Before that, and maybe because my father was playing with Ravi Shankarji, I was a happy fan of the sitar.

NMK: What about the sound of the shehnai?

ZH: The shehnai is a very difficult instrument to play and can sound terrible if it is played badly. There was an in-joke among us musicians about a line in the song '*Aap ke nazron* *ne samjha'*. The line goes like this: '*Har taraf bajne lagin saikdon shehnaiyan.*' [A thousand shehnais started to play all around us.] And we musicians would laugh and say: '*Saikdon shehnaiyan bajne lagengi toh sar phat jaayega!*' [If a thousand shehnais started playing, we'd get a crushing headache.] [*both laugh*]

NMK: Is it all about the instrument?

ZH: That would mean taking the artist out of the equation. To me, this chain of thought has limitations. It over-conforms to the rules of tradition and does not allow for interaction between musician and instrument. There was magic when you heard Vilayat Khansahib or Bismillah Khansahib play. There are other shehnai players but has anyone heard of them before or after Bismillah Khansahib? So, is it the instrument or the musician? I have heard many fine sarod players, but their hands do not grab my heart and squeeze it like the music of Ali Akbar Khansahib.

The masters say that your relationship with your instrument should be such that the instrument will get down on its knees and ask you to do what you will of it, extract what you want— have control, command and mastery over the instrument. Then there is another chain of thought that believes that the instrument is just a modem for presenting the music.

That reminds me of a lovely incident. Ali Akbar Khansahib and Sultan Khansahib and I were once sitting in his classroom in California and he said: 'Sultan, did you bring your sarangi? Will you play something?' Sultan Bhai replied: 'Khansahib, I'm sorry, but I have left it at the hotel. I just came by to say hello.' Ali Akbar Khansahib insisted: 'We have a sarangi in our music store, let's bring it out.'

So, they brought out the sarangi and put it down. Sultan Bhai looked at it and said: 'Khansahib, this sarangi is broken. It's in a bad state. I don't think I can play it.' Ali Akbar Khansahib smiled and said in Urdu: '*Sarangi agar theek nahin hai toh kya hua? Haath toh tumhara hai*' [So what if the sarangi is in poor condition? The hand is yours.] Sultan Bhai said, 'Oh, my God,' and rushed into a corner of the room, tuned the sarangi as best as he could and started playing.

My friend Mickey Hart, who is also a musicologist, happened to be there with his Nagra tape recorder and so he recorded Sultan Khansahib playing. Two years later we released the album and, since then, Sultan Bhai and now his family have received close to $12,000 in royalties. My conclusion is it has to be the musician, not the instrument. [*both smile*]

NMK: What a beautiful story! [*After a pause*] When we hear you play, it sounds so electrifying and perfect. I cannot imagine that you make mistakes. Or do you?

ZH: Oh yeah, everybody makes mistakes. Mistakes are part of life, as real as living and breathing, but the whole point is to keep going. Try to reach the summit another time. When I made a mistake, it used to worry me, but not any more because I'm not looking at the mistake as a mistake. It's another point of view—something that I can revisit another time. That mistake is another branch, another idea.

Life is a learning experience. You're a student. You never become a master and you never will, so there's no point trying.

Do we ever find God? No. But many people seek Him. I mean, God could be the love of your life, or the best song that you've written, the best riff that you've played, or the companion that you'll never leave.

Often young tabla players say to me: 'Should I be playing Punjab gharana? But this composition from this other gharana is so nice too.' I tell them: 'There's no such thing as wrong, it's just different. That's all it is. Use it in your playing. Don't think of it as wrong. If you do, you're limiting your experience.'

NMK: But I am sure you still strive for perfection.

ZH: I do. It motivates me to get up every day, it gets me on to the stage again and again—because if you're not looking for something, what's there in life? It's part of the creative process. I always say, music dies each night and is reborn the next day. *'Ek shamma jali, parwana uda, taiyyar hui, taiyyar hua.'* The parwana [moth] will burn, and yet it will be drawn to the flame again the next day.

Perfection is something you'll never attain. But it doesn't matter if I don't attain it, at least I have tried.

NMK: Your father heard you play over the years; was he generous in giving praise?

ZH: No, not at all. An occasional 'hmm'. That's pretty much it.

One night when I was a kid, I was sleeping in my room and must have got up to get a glass of water or something and I overheard Abba and Amma talking. He was saying to her: *'Kabhi tumhara Zakir aisa kuchh kar jaata hai stage pe, ke main hairaan ho jaata hoon ke yeh kahaan se aaya.'* [Sometimes your

Zakir plays in such a way on stage that I'm taken aback. I ask myself from where did this come?] I think Abba wanted to share his joy and his sense of pride with my mother. He did not want to say it to my face. I just happened to overhear him.

Abba was often very critical, especially when I agreed to certain projects—'What is this? Why are you doing this? It's not you.' I tried to explain to him that it was all a learning process. I needed to see if it had anything for me. If not, that was fine and I'd just move on. I wanted to discover things for myself. If I was going to play with John McLaughlin, for example, I had to learn about jazz.

Abba never really stopped me from doing anything, but he wanted to make sure that I did not forget who I was, and that I had an identity and should not lose it.

NMK: Your father love experimenting too. It is well known that he was the first tabla player to record an album with the great Buddy Rich. Their groundbreaking album was appropriately called *Rich a la Rakha*. So, he must have loved jazz too.

ZH: Yes, jazz is a cousin form to Indian classical, as I've mentioned. Abba liked jazz and had many friends from the jazz world visiting him in Bombay.

NMK: I must quote a wonderful comment about your father by Mickey Hart: 'Allarakha is the Einstein, the Picasso; he is the highest form of rhythmic development on this planet.' Your father made history in so many ways, including changing the way tabla players were regarded in India, elevating their status.

ZH: That is right. Earlier tabla players were basically non-entities when it came to receiving any attention in a performance. Their names did not appear in ads, and LP and EP record covers did not list their names. When it came to their remuneration, as we discussed, it was a tenth of what the lead artist was paid. Of course, we had tabla ustads like Thirakwa Khansahib, Amir Hussain Khansahib, Pandit Kanthe Maharajji and Habibuddin Khansahib, who were occasionally presented in a solo baithak, or had a twenty-minute solo performance at a music festival, but there was never any focus on tabla players as being an equally important part of a classical concert.

In the 1950s, there emerged three very important instrumentalists: Ustad Ali Akbar Khansahib, Pandit Ravi Shankarji and Ustad Vilayat Khansahib. We have discussed these masters many times in this book, and it was these same people who saw the merit in developing a dialogue-oriented performance with their accompanying tabla players—they believed in the potential appeal that this would have. And, fortunately for them, the tabla players, whom we refer to as the holy trinity of our tradition—Ustad Allarakha Khansahib, Pandit Samta Prasadji and Pandit Kishan Maharajji—emerged around the same time.

They were magical tabla players. They were exciting to watch, they thrilled audiences all over India with their control of laya, taal, and impressive sound production and dizzying speed. They had an electrifying presence on stage and knew how to capture the audience's attention. These great tabla players became the partners and preferred accompanists of the three great instrumentalists mentioned above. Together they created music of high energy and intensity whilst presenting a vastly entertaining interaction.

Suddenly there came a new-found respect for the tabla, and the recognition of its importance on the concert stage followed. In fact, audiences would demand to know the name of the tabla accompanist before buying a ticket; so organizers sometimes hired one of these great tabla players even before booking the artist they were to accompany. Their solo performances became very popular, and thus elevated the status of the tabla and the tabla players.

We owe everything to these giants; without their existence and Herculean efforts perhaps we tabla players would still be in the shadows. All their hard work made it possible for us to reap the rewards, both commercially and socially.

NMK: In terms of the tabla repertoire, did it always have one of its own?

ZH: When the tabla found its way into the world of classical music, it did not have its own repertoire to draw upon, and so it ended up adopting and transposing the pakhawaj repertoire as its source material. Most gharanas eventually moved away from the pakhawaj and came up with a language that was a hybrid of the pakhawaj and the local drums of the region where the tabla players lived. Punjab and Benares found ways to adopt more of the pakhawaj repertoire and develop a fluid technique to comfortably execute those compositions on the tabla.

Take the Punjab gharana [tabla]; it has maintained close ties to the pakhawaj. We students have all studied the ancient language and compositions in this system, and were even encouraged to take up the pakhawaj as part of our initial taleem [training] before we moved exclusively to the tabla.

My father's guru, Mian Qadir Baksh, was a pakhawaj player and it is said that a majority of the rhythm players in Punjab were Mian-ji's students.

NMK: I believe your close friend Mickey Hart studied tabla with your father, and then you worked with him on the now famous album *Planet Drum*. How did that come about?

ZH: *Planet Drum* is basically a link in a chain of events. Mickey Hart and I had begun working together in 1974-75. The music ensemble that I started in 1973 was renamed the Diga Rhythm Band and Mickey and I produced an album called *Diga*. Warner Brothers released the LP in the mid-1970s. It was the very first world rhythm ensemble, and featured drummers from India, the USA, the Middle East, Latin America, Africa and other parts of Asia. No one had thought of doing this before.

The relationship between Mickey and me strengthened from that time, and we decided that we would find like-minded rhythmists from various parts of the world and see if we could somehow spark an interest in the importance of rhythm. This led to different attempts, including the *Rhythm Devils*. But the spark really happened when the book *Drumming at the Edge of Magic: A Journey into the Spirit of Percussion*, written by Mickey Hart, Jay Stevens and Fredric Lieberman, was published in 1990. The book accompanied the album *At the Edge*, and, in the book, Mickey explored the origins of drumming. There was also a chapter in it talking about my work, and where I came from, etc. The book was a huge success, and so was the accompanying CD. It had tracks by like-minded rhythmists from Nigeria, Brazil and Afro-Cuban traditions. This attracted interest in what we were doing as rhythm players, so we could record the album *Planet Drum*.

We all believe this is a rhythm planet. So, the idea was to show that rhythm is in everything, and even the earth revolves around its axis at a particular rhythm; the solar system works in rhythm—the whole idea was rhythm.

Babatunde Olatunji, the senior statesman rhythm maestro from Nigeria, the Brazilian Shaman drummer Airto Moreira, and I got together with Mickey Hart. Each of us brought another rhythmist to the mix. Airto asked Giovanni Hidalgo and his wife Flora, a singer, to join us; Baba Olatunji brought Sikiru Adepoju, who was another Nigerian talking-drum maestro, and I asked T.H. Vinayakram from India. That made a very substantial group of people.

We co-produced and recorded *Planet Drum*. We did everything. The recording took only seven days. Mickey, the engineer Tom Flye and his assistant Jeff and I threw ourselves into the post-production and a month later we emerged bleary-eyed with the PD master. When the album was released, it topped the world music category for some twenty-six consecutive weeks and sold almost a million records. At that point, the Grammy Awards did not have a category for world music. When *Planet Drum* was about to come out, in 1992, they introduced a 'Best World Music Album' award and we were the first to win it.

My father and guru, and his two colleagues, who were the holy trinity of the tabla, initiated this fight for drummers to be recognized, and to a certain extent *Planet Drum* fulfilled their vision. It is an out-and-out rhythm recording and, as a percussionist myself, it is a well-deserved nod to the importance of rhythm.

Planet Drum was not a one-time project; it triggered a huge interest in rhythm and fanned the popularity of drum-and-bass hip-hop, rap and beat music, all of which came from rhythm-based music. As these forms started to emerge, rhythms became a very important element in a recording. It has now got to a point where most hip-hop and rap artists ask their music producers to send them a beat so that they can write their songs to it, and stuff like that.

Before *Planet Drum*, you did not have that kind of interest in rhythm-based music, and so it sparked this whole new way of thinking. In that sense, *Planet Drum* remains a landmark. And then *The Global Drum Project* followed.

NMK: In the mid-1970s you were involved with Shakti. The impact of Shakti was huge and certainly helped to further the sounds of world music. It not only included musical influences of the East and the West, but also of North and South India. I remember hearing the album *A Handful of Beauty* (1976), and its title so aptly described the music. Shakti is a real milestone.

ZH: The reason Shakti is a milestone, and of personal importance to me, comes from the fact that it opened the doors to the concept of world music. It was doubly sweet because the foundation of Shakti was laid at the same time as *Planet Drum*.

Shakti is unique and unparalleled in the universe of music and it was probably the first group of its kind to have explored, without limit, the one salient feature that is common in Indian music and jazz—and that is improvisation. There were earlier attempts that combined the two systems but, as far as I know, besides the LP *Karuna Supreme*, which released in 1975 and which Ali Akbar Khansahib, John Handy and I did, all other attempts involved composed solos that were written without spontaneous improvisation.

Shakti explored the idea of spontaneous improvisation. The advantage we had was that John McLaughlin, apart from being the most versatile guitarist of his time, was also someone who had studied the Indian system of improvising. He had learned how to play the veena, and our other team member, the violinist L. Shankar, had learned about jazz harmonies and had worked with that form. As we've discussed, working extensively as a teenager with Hindi film musicians, who played all kinds of Indian and non-Indian instruments, helped me. I was also given an insight into the jazz and rock worlds by my father, who brought from his travels many records of bands like the Grateful Dead, Jefferson Airplane and the Doors. I remember Abba had me take some piano lessons as well.

The most important fact was that we, the Shakti team, were young enough to allow for musical 'sacrilege', and so we could ignore the restrictions imposed on us by our respective traditions, in the interest of finding a road towards oneness. Similarly, the connoisseurs at that time frowned upon interactions between South and North Indian musicians, but the advantage for T.H. Vinayakram, fondly known as Vikku, and me was that rhythms are universal. In addition, I had the good fortune of occasionally working with the great maestro

Palghat Raghuji, and had also come across South Indian musicians working in Indian film music. I gleaned information that would help to overcome any barrier between Vikkuji and me. We were young and game enough, and fortunately away from India and critics or so-called well-wishers, who would have been happy to give us negative advice—and so we were totally comfortable running amok on the taal road. [*smiles*]

There we were—four musicians from varied backgrounds, sitting on a stage platform in Indian style and, with complete conviction, playing music that was never heard before—it was a totally positive offering. The energy of four as one was strong. We were confident that our musical statement would become valid and accepted as a road to traverse, and that would eventually lead to what is now known as world music.

NMK: I'm sure it will come as a surprise to many that Hindi film music was an added help to you when creating music in later life. I suppose the fact that so many different instruments could be played on a song, and sound great together, must have broken down barriers. In a way, we could say Indian film music was early fusion music, involving Indian and non-Indian instruments.

But you were also saying some connoisseurs frowned upon the interaction between North and South Indian musicians. Could you expand on that?

ZH: The rhythm system in South Indian music is very organized. There is a standardized formula that lays down the way the transmission should take place. Every student studies this basic formula that uses maths as the seed idea of rhythmic improvisation.

In the North Indian system, the emphasis is more on the rhythm tradition being a language. It is therefore more of a storytelling process, so equal importance is given to the grammar and the maths enshrined in the rhythms. Because of this teaching style, there is great emphasis in the North Indian system on an individualized approach to improvisation and this has created many points of view [gharanas], rather than a single standardized approach.

Personally, I thought it was a great fit to combine the teaching systems from the North and South—and so give tabla students a teaching process that incorporates all the important points of view [gharanas] into one coherent idea. I used myself as the guinea pig and found that it was a huge learning curve for me. As a result, a much-needed dimension to my musical expression has been added.

I must thank the great Palghat Mani Iyer, Palghat Raghuji, my dear friend T.H. Vinayakram, Shri Lalgudiji, Shri Balamuraliji, L. Shankar; the lord of the mandolin, U. Srinivas, and many others for helping me to imbibe, in a minuscule way, some of the salient features of South India's rich musical tradition.

NMK: Can you talk about how much the North Indian masters influenced you?

ZH: I will try to give a very short answer to a very long and ongoing story.

I believe a teacher or mentor can instil in a tabla student all the ingredients and tools necessary for him or her to become technically efficient as a solo performer. But it is a near impossible task to impart all the improvisational abilities that would meet the potential demands that are made upon the tabla students when they accompany a lead musician. It is through assimilation that they must accumulate these skills—by listening, watching, memorizing and analysing. So, if they are able to find mentors, say, an instrumentalist, a vocalist or a dancer to bounce off their ideas, they'll reach a clearer understanding of their craft. This helps a tabla player to build confidence in the ability to cope with the demands of being an accompanist.

I had the good fortune of playing the tabla for Kathak dancers; I became an apprentice accompanist on one glorious occasion to Ali Akbar Khansahib, an apprentice accompanist to Ravi Shankarji and an accidental accompanist to the Kathak diva Sitara Deviji. All this happened before I was sixteen—a privileged student indeed—but it was not until I joined Ali Akbar Khansahib's music college in California as a teacher, and became his accompanist, that I really found my first instrumentalist mentor. It was then that I started to put my portfolio together in earnest.

The learning must continue. Reinventing one's self is an ongoing process—being in the present with an eye to the future. My growth would have remained in the shadow of Ali Akbar Khansahib's musical expression had it not been for the influences that arrived in the form of Shivkumar Sharmaji, Hariprasad Chaurasiaji, John McLaughlin and Mickey Hart. Shivji and Hariji were amazingly generous performers who were more than willing to let me try my wares on the stage and be my sounding board. It was my association with a number of these greats that helped me create my tabla identity.

Accompanist tabla players are chameleons that are both expressing themselves and reflecting the ideas that the main artist wishes to convey. If they are successful at this, they'll become the true exponents of all musical interactions. I am not sure if I will ever be that. But I must, in all humility and gratitude, say that hopefully I am what these greats envisaged, and that the lessons I've learned from them can go forward in the intended spirit. It has been a joy to learn about this wondrous art form from these fabulous practitioners.

NMK: In rereading what you've said to me, it is clear that your training and relationship with your father has been unmatched in your life.

ZH: It was very important. Look, I started off as his son and then I became his student, apprentice, colleague and finally a friend. We lived through many facets of a relationship. Yet it was obvious that he gave more than he got.

NMK: You don't think he got anything back?

ZH: He may have, but I think he gave more. I was very selfish. I took. Maybe I could have helped him become more of a man of the world.

Whenever I think of an example of purity, I visualize my father. He was not of this world. He was not made of this clay. I remember he would never worry about things. There were so many times when we sat in the semi-darkness of the Akram Terrace flat in Mahim and Amma would say: 'I only have a few rupees left. *Kal bazaar kaise hoga*? [How will we buy food tomorrow?] Abba would simply smile and say: 'Don't worry, God will provide.' And sure enough, an hour or two later, someone would arrive at our door and tell him: 'Tonight there's an impromptu music programme by Vilayat Khansahib. They want you to play. Will you come? Here's 100 rupees.' In 1958-59, a hundred rupees was a lot and so that bought us food for the next few days.

Abba was a man of God. When he started playing with Ravi Shankarji, he decided: 'He's my brother. I'll play with him and no one else.' He refused all other concerts. He did not make a zillion rupees—that did not matter to him. What mattered to him was being where he wanted to be. That made him happy. He had the kind of personality, or purity, that you talk of when you describe your impression of meeting Bismillah Khansahib—someone for whom only music mattered.

NMK: I'm assuming you have accompanied Bismillah Khan?

ZH: Yes, I have. There was a man called Bipin Bihari Sinha, a concert organizer and a friend of my father's, who asked me to play in Patna when I was about fourteen. I was too young to travel alone but Sinha Sahib promised my father that he would look after me. He was involved with a very well-known festival that took place at Dussehra, and still does. So, in 1965, I went with Sinha Sahib to Patna and played tabla with the musicians that he had invited. One year I was accompanying Shivkumarji, and another year it was Pandit Jasrajji. At a private gathering I even got the chance to play the tabla for Begum Akhtar. Her regular tabla player, Mohammed Ahmed Khansahib, had to return home because of some family issue, so I was asked to play. After the evening's proceedings were over, there was a gathering where she sang. Many musicians were present.

It was also in Patna that I first accompanied Bismillah Khansahib and then again here in Malabar Hill at a wedding of a very rich businessman. But the opportunities of accompanying him became rare because his son Nazim started playing the tabla for him, and there was another guy on the nagara. So, Bismillah Khansahib had no need for anyone else.

NMK: You mentioned earlier that you do not play at corporate events or at weddings, so was playing at this wedding with Bismillah Khan an exception?

ZH: In my early years as a musician I took every job that came to me. Did I tell you that as a young kid I once had to wait in the kitchen before we were led into the sitting room to play for some rich folk? That's how it was sometimes in the old days.

I was aware of all these corporate events that took place in some hotel ballroom and were usually private gatherings for company clients and employees. They would book an artist to perform and then a lavish dinner would be served. At first it seemed that they were supporting musicians, giving them work. It then got to a point that these private events were in fact taking away sponsorship from public concerts because the corporate world felt they were already doing something, so there was less and less financial support for public events.

I was once in Calcutta for a concert, *Heat and Dust* had been released, so I was already a face, socially accepted by the higher echelons. I was invited to a wedding of a rich family. We were all standing around on a huge lawn and I noticed at the end of the lawn there was a stage and from a distance I could see some musicians playing. I could hear they were playing the sitar and the shehnai very well, so I drifted over there and found that the musicians were none other than Bismillah Khansahib and Vilayat Khansahib. Guests were walking up and down the lawn, some people were eating, kids were running around and most people were talking. I felt so angry and so sad. I had tears in my eyes that something like this could happen to these great musicians.

On that day, twenty-seven years ago, I decided that I would not play at weddings and corporate events. I would just do concerts. I don't do concerts that are sponsored by tobacco or alcohol companies either. It's just something I won't do. But I do play for friends. For example, Sultan Khansahib and I played at Sumantra Ghosal's fiftieth birthday because we're close friends. We surprised him and played in Pooh's [Ayesha Sayani] house. It was fun. But that's a different thing.

NMK: Did you talk to Bismillah Khan about music or were you too young?

ZH: He talked and we listened. When he came to Bombay, he always stayed on Grant Road in a very Muslim-style old hotel. '*Humko toh yahaan theek hai, khana peena achchha hai, do room hain*' [This place suits me, the food is good and we have two rooms]. He and his ten family members stayed in those two rooms. The organizers would suggest that he stayed at the Taj Mahal Hotel, but Khansahib would insist: 'No, no, this hotel is fine. The food is good here.' During his stay in Bombay, he would play at the IMG festival, the Nehru Centre, Shanmukhananda Hall and then return home to Benares.

I liked the sound of his shehnai. Whether it was the way he had the reeds or the way he controlled the blow into the reeds, I don't know, but he created a very blissful and musical sound. His tonality remains unmatched. When you hear other shehnai players, the tone springs out at you. With Khansahib it flowed out and was a very sweet and pleasing, embracing tone.

The shehnai used to be part of the naubat or ensemble of instruments played at royal courts. Bismillah Khansahib took the shehnai from there and brought it to concert halls that had great status all over the world. That is something very special. That's why Bismillah Khansahib is Bismillah Khansahib. We have not heard of any other shehnai player after him.

Another reason he became famous in India was thanks to the movie *Goonj Uthi Shehnai*, in which he played the shehnai. The film became a very big hit and he became a household name, just like the Taj Mahal tea ads helped to make me famous in India.

NMK: They certainly did! When we met in Pune recently, the man at the hotel desk asked whom I had come to see, and when I said your name, he got all excited and said: 'Wah, Taj!' [*both smile*]

You recently celebrated your birthday. Are there things that you would have liked to talk to your father about at this stage in your life?

ZH: We had a very fulfilling relationship. When I had to travel more frequently, we would talk on the phone, joke, laugh—talk about the movies and things. But I have a feeling the father-and-son relationship sort of stopped when he started to teach me. My passion for the tabla was what got a reaction out of him—that drew his attention, so if I did well, we had time together.

NMK: Was playing music a way of getting his attention and approval?

ZH: It probably was. When you have a larger-than-life figure like Abba in your living room, you want to make sure that every now and then his gaze falls upon you. You want an acknowledgement that you're someone special, and he made me feel special.

My father and then my wife Toni—these two relationships are key to my life. My relationship with my mother also played a big role in shaping the person that I am. Amma has a lot to do with that.

NMK: In terms of a formal education, your Wikipedia page says that you studied at St Xavier's College in Bombay. Is that right?

ZH: That was just for a little while, because I had to go on tour to Europe. There was a blinkered kind of an academic world in India in those days. You had three categories to choose from: arts, science or commerce, and that was it. You didn't have a course on ethnomusicology or anything like that. It did not exist, and it still doesn't, although I hear there is some change in these areas of study.

NMK: Do you think it would have been useful to have a PhD?

ZH: It doesn't really matter to me. But it does matter in academic circles. I have been asked to teach as a visiting professor in the humanities department at Princeton, Stanford and Berkeley. Yet I know they would hesitate to give me a permanent position because I don't have a PhD, and have not been published.

It's partly because they rely on funding and it looks good when you have people on your staff who are Dr So-and-So, Nobel prize winners, etc. So, in the academic world, degrees matter. But people who want to learn the tabla are not interested in whether I have a degree or not.

My daughter Anisa studied film at UCLA, while getting her BA, and I asked her why she decided not to study any further. She said: 'Dad, I am getting the chance to work in a film unit as an associate producer. It's a big experience for me.' What she meant was that practical experience, especially in films, has greater value than a college degree in cinema studies.

Anisa worked on the 2005 film *Waterborne*, in which Shabana Azmi had a role. It's an English-language film that was shot in California. Anisa was the one who made sure the film was on schedule and on budget. She has worked as a line producer on several films.

NMK: Do your daughters live near you?

ZH: Anisa and her husband, Taylor Phillips, live in Los Angeles, which is an hour's flight away or a six-hour drive from our home. Taylor works in film and television production. He was First AD on *Lost*, *Hawaii Five-O*, *Scorpion*, and the new series of *Fargo*. He was recently working on a film with Sally Field and Kelsey Grammer.

They have a beautiful baby, Zara, who was born on 30 June 2015. I am a grandfather! Lovely Zara lights up my world these days. She was walking at nine-and-a-half months. Now she's running, and we have to keep up with her. She says a few words here and there, 'Mama' or 'book'. Anisa stopped working for a while, but now she has started again and is editing and filming some documentaries.

Isabella has her own flat, which is a ten-minute drive from where we live. She is very busy teaching ballet and Salsa. She is also a stage choreographer for musical theatre and has recently worked on *Kiss Me Kate* and *The Pajama Game*, in which she also performed. Before that she was working on *Fiddler on the Roof*. She's a very responsible kind of person. I know her line of work is a struggle, but I'm very happy that both my daughters are in creative fields.

Anisa and Isabella enjoy visiting India. They speak a little Hindi, but not too much. Because I was always travelling, and the little time I had with them, I did not want to spend time teaching them Hindi, so we spoke in English. The Ali Akbar College of Music has started a Hindi course, so Toni and Isabella have attended classes there. Anisa too.

NMK: What's it like being a grandparent?

ZH: It's the best thing ever for both Toni and me. You look at your granddaughter and you think there is no one like her, she's the smartest and cutest kid in the whole wide world. At the same time, I know I'm biased.

I never thought that I would feel that life could begin again and it has. It's like going into this little cocoon and coming out fifty years younger, in mind and thought. You feel a renewed vigour about living. And that feeling has come from my granddaughter, and that same feeling came from my daughters when they were born. It was great to put them in their strollers and take them for a walk. I would hold my head up high and think: 'Look at me with my daughters!' I would say hello to everyone who passed by, eager to share the joy that I felt. I could talk about them all the time—I felt the same way when I first started playing music. I thought that it was the best toy I ever had. I was eager to share my passion and it's much the same thing when it comes to my granddaughter; probably even more so.

NMK: I am sure you want to be around your granddaughter as she grows up. America is clearly your permanent home. Was it difficult for you and Toni to buy your first house?

ZH: Absolutely. We only managed it twenty-two years ago. It's not a big house, but it has charm. We wanted a separate dining room, a separate living room and three bedrooms. Most houses in America are kind of open plan with the living room and kitchen combined. We wanted the old style, so we looked for a Spanish stucco type of house.

It took us two years to find something that we liked. The house we finally bought is in San Anselmo, and it was built in 1927 with a deep old-style foundation. California is in an earthquake zone, and so having a strong house means hopefully it will not shake too much if there is a tremor.

San Anselmo is a beautiful, sleepy little town. George Lucas lives there and *Star Wars* and *Indiana Jones* were created there.

In the middle of the town, there is a small park with statues of Yoda and Indiana Jones. Many musicians, artists and filmmakers live nearby.

NMK: You were involved in film too.

ZH: I have acted in two movies, Sai Paranjpye's *Saaz* and James Ivory's *Heat and Dust*. The films came to me in an emergency situation—casting at the eleventh hour, and so I could not find anyone to coach me. When I was very young I used to watch Indian films. But, you know, I have not seen a single Hindi movie for twenty-six years. I don't know why, they just do not interest me. I haven't even seen *Saaz*.

Indian popular cinema caters to more or less 900 million people. Whether the lead character is from a small town, or a gangster or a romantic guy, he has to fit into a certain image of the hero. In Hollywood, when you portray a character, you are not dictated to by the definition of a hero that millions of Americans may share. How a Hollywood actor sees the character and how he or she wishes to interpret the role are up to them and the film director. So, that changes things.

NMK: Do you mean that the Hindi film hero is largely an archetype and that matters above all to audiences?

ZH: That's right. No matter how squeaky you look, you must appear on screen as a real man. So, the actor tries to make sure that those 900 million people watching him will say: 'Yeah! This is a hero!' The guy in Kanpur must say it, and the guy in Jhumri Telaiya must feel it.

There are certain Indian actors who do everything to make things look dramatic; and then there are others who present themselves as ordinary folk on the screen. I think natural acting is more difficult than making things seem larger than life. Dilip Kumar Sahib is one of the greatest actors in Indian cinema, whilst Balraj Sahni was just being a normal guy on screen. When he played a farmer, he was a farmer. When he played a police inspector, he was a police inspector. He never overpowered the scene but allowed realism to come through. That is important, but it's not what Indian audiences seem to want.

I am reminded of a funny incident that happened to me in Madras about nine years ago. At the end of the concert, a film director came to the dressing room and said: 'I want you to act in my movie.' I replied: 'Hindi movie or English movie?' 'Tamil movie.' 'But sir, I don't speak Tamil.' 'Not a problem, we can dub you.' 'I don't have much acting experience.' 'Not a problem, but can you dance and fight?'

Those were the two criteria that were important to him. It did not matter if I could act, or if I could speak Tamil, all that mattered was whether I could dance and fight! [*both laugh*]

NMK: Is there a film that makes you think—oh my God, this is amazing!

ZH: That would be *Citizen Kane*. It is a film I really enjoyed.

NMK: Which recent Hollywood film have you found uses music in an unusual way?

ZH: *Birdman*. The main instrument they used was the drum—dead sounding, no pitch, no tone, and no melody. The sound designer edited the drumming in a way that it became the film's emotive voice—I never imagined that was possible.

The other film that had a powerful and subtle score was *Gravity* with Sandra Bullock. It has a very imaginative score. The story takes place in outer space, so how to incorporate space into the music? In *2001: A Space Odyssey*, you had this big symphonic sound, but in *Gravity* they skilfully brought the silence of space into the music.

In 2000, the famous artist M.F. Husain Sahib was making his film *Gaja Gamini*, and he asked me if I would do the background music. My reaction was: 'Oh, what an honour! Which studio do you want us to work in? What kind of instrumentation would you like?' 'I only want the tabla.' I suddenly became apprehensive: 'Two hours of film with just tabla—all the way through?' That didn't make sense to me.

So, I stepped back and said I was sorry, I did not think I was ready to do that. He went ahead with one of my students, the daughter of a friend of his. So, the film had a full score of tabla, apart from a song by the composer Vanraj Bhatiaji.

NMK: You have also composed film music—a medium in which music is a part of a visual experience and not a purely aural one. What must you bear in mind when composing for images?

ZH: Film music is there to articulate the movement of what is transpiring on the screen. It could be people walking from left to right, or looking at each other, or to underscore a close-up. Everyone has a different point of view about this, but for me the responsibility of a film score is to be like water in a flower vase. The water must not only hold the flowers in place, but also nurture them. That's what music has to do for the narrative, and that's why background music is the most difficult part.

Not all the old Indian music directors composed the background score, you know. They would think: 'Dhun bana di aur phir arranger ko khada kar diya, ke bhai isko orchestra mein zara distribute kar do' [The tune is composed, now the arranger should orchestrate it].

The two composers that I personally knew who composed the background music as well as the songs were Pyarelalji of Laxmikant–Pyarelal, and Pancham-da [R.D. Burman]. They made sure that the background music was the way it should be.

Hollywood composers usually do certain types of movies. John Williams, for example, scores the big blockbusters like *Superman* and *Star Wars*. Danny Elfman and Maurice Jarre are very interesting composers. I enjoyed hearing Jarre's music in *Jacob's Ladder*. It was a very disturbing film and his score helped to create that disturbing atmosphere. Bernard Herrmann has created amazing music in *Vertigo* and *Psycho*. They are excellent films.

Good film directors use music only when a scene needs lifting; that's when the impact is stupendous.

NMK: What for you is a good example of a great film soundtrack?

ZH: John Williams's score for *Jaws*—the characters are talking and there is no music, and then suddenly the sound of a tuba announces the menacing predator. That's how to use music in a film like that. When you hear it, it should jump out at you, grab you and drag you into the water with the shark.

The score for *Jaws* is extraordinary; it's an alternating pattern of two notes, E, F—*da ra da ra da ra*—and then a third note, D, is introduced. That's all it is.

In old films, background music was there only when needed. Composer Richard Robbins of the Merchant–Ivory team used music when called for. But watch any recent commercial Hollywood film and there is constant music, or a zillion bits of ambient noise—whoosh, whoop or whatever. Somehow it has become necessary to engage the audience in more ways than just the visuals.

NMK: You were the music director for all the Indian music in Bertolucci's *Little Buddha*. How did you meet this great Italian director? Were you keen on composing for films?

ZH: I do not compose for many films. I only do them when there's time and if someone asks me. I don't have an agent out there looking for film jobs.

As far as *Little Buddha* goes, I was in California and got this call from a professor of music in Los Angeles and he asked me a couple of questions about the music in Buddha's time and I said: 'Oh yeah, probably this kind of instrument was used, etc.' Nobody really knows what the music was then—it's a myth really. I told him what I imagined it could be. The question of the film had not come up. He thanked me and hung up.

The next day the professor called back and said: 'I asked you those questions because Bernardo Bertolucci is just finishing *Little Buddha* and they are putting music to the film in London and want someone to authenticate the music of that era.' He asked if I was willing to fly to London for three days, listen to the existing background score and put forward my suggestions. I was not doing much at that time, so I agreed.

I arrived in London two days later and met Bertolucci. We watched the film and I told him what I thought about the music. Off the cuff he asked me: 'What do you think should go here?' I had my tape recorder with me with some music tracks on it, so I hooked it up to the TV monitor, we rolled up to the scene and then I lined up the music and played it: 'How about something like this?' I played two or three different tracks for him.

Then he asked: 'Can you extend your stay for a week?' And that's how I ended up working on the *Little Buddha* score. But the icing on the cake was working with Ryuichi Sakamoto. Sakamoto is a well-known Japanese composer who had worked with Bertolucci on four or five films, including *The Last Emperor*. He is also an actor.

A day or so later, we started recording at Angel Studios with the London Philharmonic Orchestra. They charged about £86,000 for two days. We played some of the music on a keyboard for Bernardo. Then the sheet music was laid out and the musicians started to play. First scene—fine, second scene—fine.

Numbers usually identify a background score: Music 1, Music 2, Music 3, etc. These are known as cues. If there are eighty-six cues in a film, you know where the music will be placed, according to the number. Thirty-four cues were planned for the orchestra on the first day. Some music pieces were ten seconds long, others fifteen seconds, and the longest piece was about forty seconds. Towards the end of the second day, we got to cue 23 or 24. Bernardo was listening to the music and suddenly said: 'No, this is not working.'

Ryuichi Sakamoto and I were perplexed and asked him: 'Bernardo, what's the problem?' 'It's just not right, it's not the way I had imagined it.' We did it all over again, and in the process, we went overtime, and so the £86,000 became £94,000. But he was still not happy. It did not matter to him that money was being spent. Eventually, Bernardo said: 'Maybe I am overdoing it. Here is Buddha, deep in meditation, trying to understand what nirvana is, and I am adding grandiose music to underscore an intimate experience.'

Believe me, even after spending all that money, he asked us to use one cello and one flute—Rakesh Chaurasia played the flute. So, the same composition that the orchestra was playing with all the harmonies, etc., ended up being played on just cello and flute.

We rehearsed the piece and came up with the melodic stuff that needed chiselling. We then played it as the film was projected on the screen. Before anyone could say anything, Bernardo said: 'Now take the same two instruments and re-record cues 12, 15 and 18 with cello and flute.' He had edited the whole film in his head. It did not matter to him that all the orchestra were just sitting around. He did not feel compelled to use them, nor did he think of the rising costs. Neither was he afraid of abandoning a grand heavenly sound that was originally planned for the scene in favour of the simple sound of the cello and flute. No, he would use what worked for the film.

NMK: He must have wanted the scene to evoke stillness.

ZH: Yes. But originally he had thought there should be a million voices inside Buddha's head—he is struggling to empty himself of all excess baggage, so that he could zero in on the light or whatever. So, that's why the orchestra—the million voices. When we were trying it out on the keyboard, it sounded all right, but when the full orchestra played the music, it did not match the mood of the scene, and Bernardo did not want to turn his film into yet another Hollywood extravaganza.

Bernardo had made the right decision. But what really amazed me was that he knew exactly which cues he wanted to re-record. He knew the story inside out—he had lived with it for a long time. You learn from his kind of focus. If I look inside myself or you look inside yourself, there is always some sort of doubt and uncertainty. When I get on to the stage, even now, I am not sure what's going to happen. When I get off the stage I'm like—was it okay?

A true learning experience is seeing someone like Bernardo Bertolucci who has vision, knows exactly what he wants, is in total command of his craft, and can tell you with full confidence: 'This is it.'

NMK: You give me the impression of being a decisive person too.

ZH: If there's something that matters to me, something that has a very unique place in my heart, it is not easy for me to take a snap decision. Otherwise I decide things quickly. I think it's because I was not raised with the idea that leading a musician's life is conquering Mount Everest. Learning and playing music was a daily routine, an everyday event. I practised, played cricket and gilli danda, went to school and came home—'*Arey Zakir, aa khaana kha le. Khaana-waana kha liya?*' [Zakir, come here and eat. Have you already eaten?] It was just a normal life. It was not as though I had to bathe, chant mantras and then sit down to play the tabla. It was never like that. The simplicity of the whole process was instilled in me from a very young age. Tabla playing was woven into my life.

NMK: You said you had many friends when you were growing up in Mahim. Do you make friends easily?

ZH: As a young man, I spent so much time with my father and was so taken up with music that nothing else really mattered. I was lucky to have travelled the world, and had the opportunity of learning so many things.

As far as my friends go, I still meet some of my school chums from the Mahim days. I have occasionally visited my old school. Most of the teachers were around till about twelve years ago and now they are gone. I have a few friendships that have lasted for over forty years. Those whom I am proud to call friends are in it for the long haul. There's Mickey Hart, Shivkumarji, Hariprasadji and John McLaughlin. They are not just music colleagues, but are more like family. We spend time together doing stuff—let's go to a movie, let's go for a drive, let's have some chaat.

There are also lots of friendships that have fallen apart because of disagreements and disappointments: 'Oh, you did not help me, or support me when I said something, you just stood by.' Sometimes other problems have occurred, and I realized it was unfair of me to try moulding people. I've learned to respect the fact that people think differently than I do.

NMK: What about Twitter and Facebook?

ZH: I'm bad with Facebook. I enjoy tweeting. It's the quickest way to keep in touch, with just one line. But Twitter is a poor substitute for a one-on-one personal relationship. It's just strumming the strings and keeping the chord humming.

I tweet my friends and the people that I work with like John McLaughlin, Shivkumar Sharmaji, Rahul Bose, the drummers Antonio Sanchez, Eric Harland, and the saxophone player Charles Lloyd. Tweeting is a way of knowing what's going on in their lives and vice versa. Sumantra Ghosal is a friend but I don't see him every day. Niladri Kumar and Rakesh Chaurasia are very dear to me, but I don't see them every day. You're a friend, but I don't see you every day. [*laughs*]

NMK: Have you lost friends because they've wanted you to help them get a recording contract or a concert? Because you're in a position of some influence and power in the music world.

ZH: Yes, that has happened. There have been worse situations than that, where I've had to be honest and say, 'No, musically you don't have it.' You look for those hands that you think a person must have, in order to get through the first gate; you look for that spark or depth—and if you don't see that spark, you have to tell them. It's tough but you must tell them. Some people take it well, others don't. The ones who take it well are still friends, but I also meet the people who did not take it well.

NMK: I suppose that's one of the downsides of being influential.

You grew up among famous people. What was that like?

ZH: I suppose when you are part of a social circle it is difficult to imagine how others perceive the people within that circle. The people that my father and I knew were just simple human beings to us, even though they were the leading names in music. I grew up sitting on the laps of many talented people in India. They were uncles and aunts, Dadaji and Nanaji, to me. Today it is difficult to forget that past relationship and think of them as gods. From the very start, they were special to me. I was a toddler and sitting in Asha Bhosleji's lap as my father rehearsed a song with her. She reminded me about it when we met recently. I am still close to Ashaji. She drops in or asks me over when she's cooking a meal. By the way, she's a terrific cook.

NMK: Back in the 1960s and '70s, the world of music in the West was associated with drugs and alcohol. How did you deal with it?

ZH: In the early years, I was living on a ranch owned by the Grateful Dead, and they were experimenting with various stimulants, but I was just involved with music and not the whole scene. There were these guys called Owsley and Wavy Gravy and, during a concert, they would give out stuff to the audience. Wavy Gravy—now that's a name! He's still around. I think he's in his eighties.

NMK: Do you think drugs and alcohol are less prevalent in the music world now?

ZH: Are you kidding? Didn't somebody die of an overdose not long ago? Amy Winehouse? Natalie Cole died before her time because her body had suffered from substance abuse.

NMK: And in India? I think it was more about alcohol.

ZH: When I was about nine years old, my father would take me with him to these addas in Bombay. I would drink Coca-Cola, and sit there, while these great musicians drank and talked music. I learned a lot about music during those evenings and I learned how to interact with musicians by watching them at the adda.

NMK: An adda can mean a place where people gather to talk. Can you explain the addas you are talking about? I think you mean the addas that opened in the 1950s during prohibition.

ZH: Yes. In Bombay and in other Indian cities you had to have a drinking permit to buy liquor and you could get one if you paid someone because you were rich, or you were a foreigner. Foreigners were allowed to buy alcohol. Otherwise alcohol was prohibited and so people would go to these 'addas' to drink. They were places hidden away in narrow back lanes where moonshine was sold—speakeasies of sorts. By and large, Catholic families ran these addas and that's why some were called 'Aunty's adda'.

Abba never drank in the day. Sometimes when he and his friends had finished recording or playing a concert, they would go in a group to a place in Mahim to drink and to eat fried fish. There was also a place in Khar Danda where they would spend the evening. Linking Road did not exist back then and for the most part it was a mosquito-infested marshland.

After the first drink or two, the mood would be just right. The film composer Madan Mohanji would sing a song that he had recorded earlier that day, and everybody would praise or critique it. The composer/vocalist Laxman Prasad Jaipurwaleji would also sing and say: 'I just made this up, it's based on such and such raga.'

The musicians would speak of their work in progress and there was an incredible sense of freedom that dominated the evening. Suddenly these quiet, reserved ustads became free human beings with no inhibitions. Drinking relaxed everyone. Sometimes Abba would make me recite rhythms (bols) that he had taught me. I would be on display and I was happy. If I did something right, an extra bottle of Coca-Cola and another fish fry would be my reward.

But when the evening would drag into the early hours, and there was more and more merriment, I would get sleepy and fed up. I was a child and impressionable and, as a result, it put me off drinking and smoking. I was never drawn to either. But if someone were to offer me a glass of a terrific Barolo, I'd happily accept. [*both smile*]

NMK: You once said you've had your share of struggles. What was your greatest struggle?

ZH: I could be bursting the bubble of an incredible myth that music is built around when I tell my students: 'We don't know what existed 150 years ago, because there are no recordings or documentation. So just stick to what's in front of you, and don't get bent out of shape.'

Many people get awestruck by the task of playing a simple rhythm. Maybe it's because they have been told it's an uphill struggle. I have seen maestros totally dampen a student's excitement by saying: 'You have to practise eighteen hours a day for twenty years before you can sing a correct note.' Who would want to get involved with something like that in this day and age? It's ironic that the maestro would even say such a thing because many ustads were themselves playing or singing professionally as teenagers. Why say you need twenty years to sing a correct note? It doesn't make sense. Contradictions are everywhere.

NMK: Are there many books on Indian classical music that are considered key?

ZH: We have a very interesting situation in North Indian classical music—our rulebook was written by a man called V.N. Bhatkhande. He spoke about 10 parent ragas known as thaats. So, you can say that such-and-such raga belongs to Kalyan thaat, or another belongs to Bhairav thaat. Bhatkhande laid it all out—this is a morning raga, this is an afternoon raga. This raga has the same notes as the morning raga, but the way you play makes it an evening raga. Bhatkhande was the one who created this system of classification. It's not a perfect system, but it has its uses.

Purists liked the idea of adhering to Bhatkhande's rulebook, but what is interesting is that he was not a performing musician himself. He was educated, whilst most musicians were not. I think the masters were referring to Bhatkhande's book when they said: '*Kitaab ka gaana bajana ek cheez hai, aur stage ka gaana bajana aur cheez hai*' [Performance by the book is one thing, performing on the stage is another]. It suggests being an academic performer is one thing but being a performer-performer is something else.

In a subtle way, the masters were possibly hinting that his words were theoretical and applying that theory to performance could be tricky to negotiate. The discussion is still on, but there are those who say: 'Oh, this raga is not being sung properly because according to Bhatkhande's book, it's supposed to be this way.' And the maestro will say: 'Come on, really? What happens to spontaneity? What happens to emotional content?'

NMK: I was very happy to have the opportunity of observing you teach—or rather, hearing you mentor—about forty tabla players at the South Bank in London. You started by quoting a comment by Miles Davis: 'Less is more.'

ZH: 'Less is more.' I was telling the students that the road to tabla nirvana is not strewn with five million compositions. I have played the same few qaidas all my life—a qaida is a composition with a pre-composed theme. I have not done anything vastly different. I know other qaidas, but this is what I am comfortable with.

NMK: When I hear you play, there is such speed and precision and inventiveness that I cannot bring my head around to thinking that you're playing only a few qaidas.

ZH: That's the whole point. You can tell the same story in five million ways and you do. It's like language; everybody speaks it differently and there are umpteen ways of expressing a thought.

I play these four or five things reasonably well and people like them, but it's up to me to inject a little bit of mystery when playing, so that it does not appear to be the same old thing. All of us tabla players, including myself, rely on a stock set of qaidas, relas, and a few chakradars and, on special occasions, unveiling a new qaida or chakradar, either recently discovered from an ancient repertoire, or newly composed—this is the modus operandi throughout our lives.

The same is true of Ahmedjaan Thirakwa Khansahib, Kishan Maharajji, Samta Prasadji or Kanthe Maharajji. If you listen to their records, the same elements reappear. They are not playing five hundred of this and a thousand of that. This is not a criticism, and it is not saying that we do not know more than we play. It is when we're on stage that we must play what we do best—play the stuff that defines us.

Vilayat Khansahib and Ravi Shankarji were known for certain ragas; the special way that Kumar Gandharvaji sang is what you wanted to hear and so he would oblige. When you listen to Anindo Bhai [Chatterjee] or Swapan Bhai [Chaudhuri], you want to hear them play the familiar—it is the telling that is slightly different each time.

We tend to talk about Indian classical music as something that is spontaneous and that we improvise and create from scratch. I think we can safely abandon that idea. We don't; we play the tried and tested.

NMK: In that case, how can students avoid being formulaic and repetitive?

ZH: What I mean is that one day you'll master what you initially did not. Technically there are certain things on the tabla that I cannot do, and other tabla players can. It's just the way my hands are shaped. I'm not going to totally avoid those things, but I'll present them in a way that does not look as though I'm floundering.

I was explaining to the students at The South Bank that it is important to build their performance around what they do best. You can move those musical phrases around, you can space them out differently, or leave them as they are—you can create many variations. And if you're trying to play something that you like, but can't, put it aside and someday you will play it.

When a student is going to give a first public performance I always ask him or her: 'Are you going to play something you like or what you can play well?' It's a decision a young musician has to make. Initially at least you should appear to be someone who has a handle on your ability at that moment in time. It doesn't mean you won't grow. All it means is that you understand your weaknesses and strengths. Novices should not assume: 'My guruji played that, so I'm going to play it.' The audience knows you are a student of a celebrated ustad, so you're putting your guruji's name to shame if you don't play well. Remember you're performing on the stage and not practising.

NMK: How would you define a good teacher?

ZH: I have noticed that most of the great maestros have students who are already at a certain level. Pandit Hariprasad Chaurasiaji, the great flautist, went to Annapurnaji after he had started performing. Nikhil Banerjee, the great sitar player, only went to Allauddin Khansahib when he was semi-professional or professional. So, they were at a level where they could inspire a great master like Baba to teach them because they had that spark.

It's hard to tell if great musicians are great teachers. If you put a beginner in front of them, they would not have the patience to walk the beginner through the first steps that a modest 500-rupees-a-class teacher would have. Teachers who do all the nitty-gritty work are good teachers too. They provide you with the basic packages. They'll tell you what you need, but they are unable to tell you what to do with all that.

NMK: I suppose it's like asking Shakespeare to teach the English alphabet!

ZH: Precisely. In a prestigious university like Princeton, you will find a full professor will not necessarily do the teaching. The assistants and associate professors teach.

Essentially a music teacher must find a way of opening the door to understanding the craft—how to put two and two together in a simple way. You can learn 500 ragas and their structure in a year, but what will you do with that knowledge? How will you bring it to fruition? Only when the building blocks are in place can your teacher point you in the right direction.

Abba taught me everything about the tabla—compositions, rhythms and, knowingly or unknowingly, he was preparing me to become a solo performer. Did that make me a good accompanist? No, because he was not teaching me how to interact with the lead musician. He did not tell me: 'There's a sitar player called Budhaditya Mukherjee, and he plays like this, so if you play the tabla with him, what will you do?'

Abba did not tell me how he played the tabla with Ravi Shankarji or Ali Akbar Khansahib, I had to listen and observe.

I had to see how they conversed. What worked and what did not. Only after I attended hundreds of concerts was I able to use the information I had gathered. I had to develop my own way of scanning the brains of the musicians I was going to accompany. Figure out their moods and feelings, what they liked and did not like and then put together a package on the fly. There are 500 sitar players, and as many ways of playing the sitar, so one cannot apply the same theory to each and every instrumentalist. How can a guru tell you all this in advance?

NMK: So, you prefer not to take on students?

ZH: You see, I grew up among musicians and saw some ustads who would accept a student at the drop of a hat. Musicians did not earn a great deal in former times, and so the guru–shishya ceremony itself provided some money. A student had to make a nazrana and offer gifts to the guru. Then the student officially became the student, but whether they got a chance to study with the master was not the issue.

My father used to say that his guru Mian Qadir Baksh had 125,000 students! I thought about it a lot and figured that if I lived ten lifetimes, I would not know 125,000 people. How was it possible for one man to teach 125,000 people?

When Abba first put his hand on the tabla to learn from Mian-ji, the guru said to him: 'That's the same way I approach and address my instrument. How did you learn that? I didn't teach you. I've never met you before.' Abba replied: 'But I have seen you.' That made me think there were 125,000 people who considered themselves students of the guru—the believers, the fans, the wannabe players, people who in their hearts and minds had accepted him as their teacher, without even studying with the ustad.

I remember when I travelled to different places with Sultan Khansahib; he would introduce me to people he said were his students. The same thing would happen in cities outside India. And I would ask: 'Khansahib, when was the last time you were in Manchester?' He said: 'I can't remember.' 'How can he be your student then? When did you teach him?' 'Oh, he came to me and I told him something.' 'Khansahib, you call this person your student, a person who has barely had a lesson from you and has been practising away from your watchful eye? God knows whether he has got it right or not. He could be going around saying he's your student, even if he has seen you once, ten years ago. What if he plays somewhere and he sucks and your musician friends hear him, they will say Sultan Khansahib does not know how to teach.' He looked at me and said: 'That's all very well, but if he sings a composition of mine, he's my student.'

It did not matter to some ustads if the students played well or badly, what mattered was the number of students they had. There were also many students of my father who could barely play because they had hardly spent time with him. That's why I hesitate to take on students, but I am happy to mentor and guide young tabla players, and I do that. I have a yearly retreat that lasts between six and ten days and usually takes place every summer in California. We rent some quiet place in the hills and from morning to night we practise together and listen to music. We analyse the problems with our playing and I guide the proceedings.

NMK: How many attend the yearly retreat?

ZH: We try to keep it to fifty, but invariably we end up having about sixty people. Beyond that number, we have to say no. Students come from India, Japan, Australia, Canada, England and Europe, and of course we have American students too.

I make it clear to them that we're all students of the tabla. I don't want them to say they're my students because, by default, they're following my father's line and could be messing it all up, so there's no point. I tell them that I can guide them because of my experience, and answer questions if I am able. Toni has videotaped many of the sessions.

NMK: Your father taught you for many years, what's that one bit of advice that you think was essential?

ZH: [*long pause*] The key advice he gave to me was to watch where the 'sum' is. In other words, if I play a rhythm cycle of sixteen beats, and the 'sum' is on the seventeenth beat, that's the first beat of the next cycle; that's where I have to arrive. Whatever rhythm cycle you play, and you're creating a thought process, a path to walk on—you must be attentive to where you'll arrive. The way he put it was: '*Sum ko dekho*' [Be mindful of the 'sum'].

Say, a guy is parachuting from a plane and he's going to land in a circle on the ground that has an X marked on it. Everyone is watching him with their mouths open and as soon as he lands on the X, there's an explosion of cheers and applause. Playing music and arriving at the point where you need to reach—the 'sum'—is something like that. You can be playing and playing and if you don't know how to round it off, you'll get nowhere. You should not be stumbling through. Your approach must be clear and smooth, so the audience knows that you are now arriving at the 'sum' and they are part of the experience of touching down. In the Western world, they call it 'the big finish'. If you have that big finish, everybody will be like 'Ah!' That's what Abba meant when he said: '*Sum ko dekho.*'

NMK: Is that the same advice you give other young musicians?

ZH: That is the best advice. The 'sum' signifies a goal, a resolve. Unless you can tie a ribbon on the statement you're trying to make, it does not complete itself.

NMK: Your father set up the Ustad Allarakha Institute of Music in Bombay in 1985 and your brother Fazal runs it. The Institute's website describes the philosophy of the school as imparting the knowledge of the tabla, particularly of the Punjab gharana. Does Fazal closely follow your father's school of playing?

ZH: I think Fazal follows it much more than I do. Because I travel around the world, I am able to use the knowledge that I was given—and like a piece of wax, I can shape it into anything that I want, so that it works well with whatever I am interacting with.

As far as Abba's school is concerned, Fazal runs it and teaches the students. Over the years, a few hundred students have studied there, but at any given time there are no more than thirty or forty. My brother has to transmit the knowledge as received by him. It is his father's school. He is very focused and very particular about providing the kind of teaching that my father would have. That responsibility rests on his shoulders.

Taufiq has chosen a different instrument altogether. He does not play the tabla, but the djembe. It's an African drum, and he has transposed my father's teachings to the djembe. Taufiq has developed a new kind of hybrid language that combines these two languages. And although he uses the same material that he has learned from Abba, the djembe is nevertheless a different instrument, so Taufiq is not really tied to protecting the information as prescribed.

My brothers are both very beautiful drummers. I have to say that it was probably a bit more difficult for Fazal because he had to follow our father and then me. For him to make his place in the world of music was tougher, but he has done it.

For Taufiq, the difficulty was to play a totally non-Indian instrument, and yet play the traditional Indian repertoire on it. He has formalized a technique of playing qaidas, relas, chakradar and paran on the djembe. Taufiq has started teaching this system to many devoted students, and who knows, there might be a whole new voice to Indian drumming. In fact, Taufiq plays other percussion instruments too, including the duff, bongos and batajon.

Both my brothers have done very well and I am so proud of them. It's fabulous. It's not easy to have three brothers in the same family who play rhythms, and for each to find his own niche. We are not stepping on each other's toes. And I am grateful to my father for encouraging us to define ourselves individually.

NMK: I believe Taufiq's wife, Geetika Varde, is a singer?

ZH: Yes, she's a classical singer. She studied with Smt. Manik Bhide. Geetika takes her singing seriously. I don't think anyone in her family is a musician, but she chose to be one. She balances her duties as wife and mother, and is very careful that she makes sure that their son, Shikhar, is well looked after. Shikhar has turned into a very decent rhythm player and is already performing on the stage. Razia Apa's son, Faizan, has also turned into a fine percussionist and composer for Bollywood films, and her daughter, Afshan, is an accomplished and award-winning film-maker.

Fazal's wife is Birwa. She is an interior designer from National Institute of Design (NID), and is also a folk dancer. She has taught dancing and is currently producing a concert series in Gujarat at the UNESCO heritage sites. That's another artist in the family. Their daughter, Alia, is studying ballet, and their son Azann is a very fine piano player. He's not even twelve. The next generation is already on the move!

I am really delighted that they are encouraging their kids to be creative. It changes a person's point of view when you have art inside of you. Your perspective on the world is quite different.

NMK: What are your thoughts on the present generation of Indian musicians?

ZH: Niladri Kumar is very good and so are Rakesh Chaurasia and Rahul Sharma—they are all very good. But it is not just hard, but also unfair of me to talk about only a few of the many talented young Indian musicians. It's true that I have been able to perform with just a few of them, but my hope is that, very soon, I will get to play with many more. There is a selfish reason on my part in wanting to work with the young geniuses, and that's because I find their view of music deeply inclusive of the sonic world in which we exist.

When I was young, the information available to me about how music was spoken in other parts of the world was very sparse. The young musicians of today have so much information at their fingertips about music. They have grown, not only learning Indian classical music, but also other relevant forms, so that their musical expression is more universal. It is an evolved understanding of all musical forms and this makes these young musicians well-rounded artists at a very young age. I envy their grasp of the many art forms and can only imagine the genius level they'll arrive at in a few years. To play with them in the near future—and, with their help, understand a new and fresh approach of improvising that incorporates a universal mindset—is an exciting thought.

*

NMK: Today's session is taking place in November 2016 in Bombay. We are meeting again after some months. You're getting ready to travel to South Africa for a concert this week. How do you prepare for the concert at such a distance?

ZH: Before you came, I was telling Nirmalaji, my secretary in India, to inform the South African promoter about my technical requirements. How much space I need on the stage, what instruments I shall bring, how many microphone lines are required, etc. I'm playing with Rakesh Chaurasia, and haven't played with him in South Africa before.

Playing in Africa is special because that's where most of the rhythm traditions in the world have come from. The drum and dance belong to Africa. I have listened to the music of many great African musicians, including Hugh Masekela and Miriam Makeba from South Africa, and the Soweto Choir. There are so many excellent African musicians—I am thinking of Oumou Sangaré from Mali and Doudou N'Diaye Rose from Senegal, who was a master of the sambar, a traditional drum. He passed away in 2015 and was one of the most respected drummers of his time. A great percussionist, Hukwe Ubi Zawose, from Tanzania, used to play many instruments and was known for a special kind of throat singing where the voice comes from the core of the main chakra, all the way through the throat and out, so it sounds like three people are singing. The Zawose family developed this particular technique, and it has stayed in this one family. Hukwe Ubi Zawose passed away recently, but his line continues. About four years ago, I invited one of his cousins, a blind singer, to perform at my father's barsi in Bombay. He was a big hit.

These are some of the musicians that I know about. Africa has a beautiful and ancient rhythm tradition. So, I cannot just walk in there and think I'm interacting with people who know nothing about rhythm. In combination with Rakesh Chaurasia, we have to try and show how the musical worlds of India and Africa might relate to one another.

NMK: Have you discussed Indian music with African musicians? I wonder what they think of it.

ZH: Absolutely. I have played and worked with all the musicians that I have mentioned. They find the tabla is beyond their understanding in some ways, because it has gone into a scientific realm where the technique has been developed and refined, and there is much training involved. Whilst of the highest calibre, the dos and don'ts in African drumming are not as rigidly exercised. Playing rhythmic instruments in Africa is very organic. What I mean by 'organic' is that it comes from the earth—it is alive in the people. Similar to qawwali singers in Ajmer, who are not trained in classical music or vocal music, but have just grown up singing qawwali. It's learned from childhood. I think the same applies to Rajasthani folk singers—they have that lilt in their voices, the quiver and flavour. A child of the Langa family in Rajasthan can sing in that style; a little kid of the Manganiyars has it—it's in their DNA. Their music is healing.

Something you will notice about qawwali singers—and the same is largely true of folk singers in Rajasthan or in the Punjab—is that they often sing in a very high voice. That's because their lives are largely spent in open fields, or on the plains and in the vast desert—they express themselves in those vast spaces—and so their voices project.

Folk singing often begins with the idea of controlling the vibrations and sonic waves so that the voice expands. For folk singers to restrict themselves to small proportions, until you get to the point where it becomes majestic, is unclear to them. In classical music, we do not do that at the start, and it is probably where we need to arrive eventually. In other words, classical singers or instrumentalists develop a raga performance note by note, gradually moving towards a grand climax, whereas a folk singer would go right to the high moment of the piece. One should be aware, of course, that the performance of a raga is a long and arduous journey, while a folk song is a short, earthy experience. Folk singers may also ask why we need to write the music down. Is it not inside of you? Are you not already aware of it when you are two or three years old? Why do you have to practise?

Take the Soweto Choir—here you have eight or twelve singers singing a harmonic projection that is no different from a symphony orchestra. Where did they learn to sing Western harmonies and four-part harmonies? The singers have not been to music school, but have probably just sat around the fire every evening and sung. Their tradition of music has come down from generation to generation.

The interesting thing is that a trained classical or semi-classical musician in India needs to have a tanpura, or some kind of pitch identifier in order to sing. Without any kind of pitch identifier, the Soweto Choir can sing and sound as one, all the harmonies in place. They are naturally tuned to the pitch. They may not immediately understand that we need to find our way in the tonal world, in the rhythm world. We need to find our way to a downbeat, where the 'sum' is—where the 'one' is—because as far as they are concerned, the 'one' is where they decide it is. You're playing and at a point you feel like stopping, you stop. It does not have to be—1, 2, 3—and you stop at 3. That's not how they think.

From the day they open their eyes, they have it. That's why folk music is something that will last forever.

NMK: Does African music not have a classical music tradition?

ZH: What do you call classical music? Any organic form of music is classical. If you're listening to a Benarsi kajri, it's classical. Or a coil recording of Gauhar Jaan singing at a gathering for the Nawab of Rampur is also classical.

Do you know, the Western world, for the most part, does not think that Indian music is classical but ethnic? It is listed as folk in the Library of Congress and the Smithsonian in Washington DC. I remember when Ravi Shankarji talked to reporters in the West, he used to insist that they understand that our music was classical music. It has a system and rules and you have to learn it in a proper way. He would hammer it in and felt that it was necessary to do so.

As far as the West is concerned, there's one form of classical music and that's Western classical music. I guess they are the ones who categorized it as classical, because their music is notated and pre-composed; it has a system that has stood the test of time—and it is standardized, so that anyone can study it. But in Indian classical music, there are as many viewpoints as there are teachers, as many opinions as there are students. When you have such disparity, such conflict and such a difference in opinion, the music is not classical, as far as the West is concerned. It's folk or some such thing.

NMK: You have performed with so many musicians. Do you still play the tabla with as many as you did in the past?

ZH: I work with fewer musicians, and am lucky that I also enjoy spending time with them. My interaction with a musician must work on many levels. We have to fight and argue and be friends and understand each other. So, I am very involved in deciding which concerts I do. I rarely accept work otherwise.

There was a time when I played a lot because I needed to—the rent had to be paid. But in the last twenty years or so, I've become a bit more selective. I find that it helps me, because if you're just a professional for hire, you may play a lot, but you are not interacting at all levels with the lead musician, and that's not very exciting. It does not nourish me. It's like being on autopilot. You go through the motions and that crushes the creative process rather than making it fly. There are times that you grow out of a professional relationship, not because you don't want to play with each other, it's just that the logistics have changed.

NMK: Have you experienced competitiveness between musicians?

ZH: Before Independence in 1947, as you know, India had several princely states and many of these had court musicians. One of the things that court musicians in almost every state would stress was that *their* music was the real thing. If a prince happened to be visiting another princely state, he would often take his musicians along, to hold a musical competition and prove that *his* musician was better than the other's. This probably happened because the musicians themselves encouraged their patrons to believe that their playing was superior by saying: 'The musicians of Rampur know nothing.'

When the princely states were abolished, the court musicians had to fend for themselves. Music had arrived on the stage, but many court musicians had no clue how to project their music to the 'aam janta', to ordinary people in rural and urban India. They were so used to performing in an intimate setting that was reserved for connoisseurs and royalty that as soon as they got on to the stage with an audience of three or four hundred, they were at a loss. So, it was the young musicians of that time like Ravi Shankarji, Vilayat Khansahib, Bismillah Khansahib and their associated tabla players, like Abba, Pandit Kishan Maharajji and Pandit Samta Prasadji, who could provide a musical experience for large audiences.

Today there is a greater camaraderie between musicians than there was years ago. As far as rhythm is concerned, it is a universal thing, so tabla players can easily accompany musicians of different schools, so there is work for all tabla players.

NMK: You mean tabla players don't compete with each other? Did you ever experience any jealousy?

ZH: They compete but only in terms of playing. It is no longer the case that if a tabla player is playing in my city, he'll be taking my job—that's not the concern. We tabla players have found a way to interact with one another and enjoy each other's company. Some of my best friends are tabla players. Shafaat Ahmed Khan, a very fine tabla player from Delhi, gave me the bass drum [the bayan] that I was playing today. He passed away a few years ago.

You ask if I experienced any jealousy? Not really. Some tabla players have even told me that because I have reached a certain level, the drag has brought them up too. If I am paid

500,000 rupees, someone who was getting 10,000 rupees will now get 50,000. There's a chain reaction and that's great.

There is no longer an issue between us tabla players. It's a beautiful thing because I remember, as a young man, observing the tension between my father and his contemporaries, to the extent that when I would go to a city where another tabla player lived, I would be told not to go to his house or to eat what he might offer me, especially sweets.

NMK: Was there a fear that you might be poisoned or something?

ZH: There was that fear. In my thirties, I had gone to play tabla in Benares with Ravi Shankarji at a festival called the RIMPA Festival. He had a huge house in Shivpur, in the suburbs of Benares, and that's where I was going to stay. At the festival, I was to accompany Ravi Shankarji, Birju Maharajji, Halim Jaffer Khansahib and another musician. When I was about to leave for Shivpur, Abba called Raviji and told him: 'Do not let Zakir go and meet such-and-such tabla player. Make sure my son is protected.'

There were stories whirling around about a tabla player's hand becoming frozen through black magic. Or another tabla player was given something to eat and he went crazy. Abba even believed that a bad spell was cast on him. He was supposed to play a duet with another tabla player, and was fine throughout the day, but in the evening, on the way to the concert, his arm suddenly went stiff. He may have just slept on his arm in a funny position, but you know how it is, there were some well-wishers who made matters melodramatic and convinced Abba: 'Something fishy has happened. You know these people are capable of doing such things.' These were the kinds of stories that prompted my father to warn Ravi Shankarji not to let me out of his sight.

I arrived at the Benares station and was taken straight to Ravi Shankarji's house and was then promptly led into a bedroom and told not to go out. But I have a different kind of nature, so I was sulking and wondering what to do. I thought to myself, why do we musicians mistrust each other? Why do we keep each other at arm's length?

Kamalapati Tripathi was the Union Minister for Railways at the time and his family home was right in the middle of Benares. His grandchildren, Abu and Anju, were friends of mine, so I called Anju and asked her to come and pick me up. Ravi Shankarji used to take a nap in the afternoon and, while he was resting, I walked to the corner of the street and waited. Anju came in her Ambassador car with its official flag; I got in and asked her to take me to Kishan Maharajji's house in Kabir Chaura.

That's precisely where I was not supposed to go. We arrived there and I knocked on the door. 'I want to meet Maharajji. *Mera naam Zakir Hussain hai.*' [My name is Zakir Hussain.] I was asked to sit down, and a few minutes later, wearing a lungi, a bare-chested Maharajji entered. He was most surprised, but also happy to see me. He greeted me with great affection—it was as though a long-lost nephew had arrived. He offered me tea and sweetmeats. I told Maharajji that Abba had asked me to pay my respects. He was moved to tears. He asked his son Pooran Maharaj to join us, and I spent an hour with them.

When I asked for permission to leave, Maharajji wanted to know where I was headed. I said I had planned to pay my respects to Samta Prasadji, the other famous tabla player. 'Haan, haan zaroor, naukar ko saath le jaao.' [Of course. Take my servant along with you, he'll show you the way.] They lived almost next door to each other but were said to be bitter enemies, despite being related and belonging to the same school of music. Samta Prasadji was in fact Kishan Maharajji's uncle.

I went over to Pandit Samta Prasadji's house and there was no problem there either. He was wearing a gamchha and greeted me warmly: 'Wonderful! you've come home!' All it needed was somebody to take the first step to break the ice. As a result, when Kishan Maharajji visited Bombay a few months later, he came over to our house. Abba and I were out that day, so he met my mother and said that he had come to pay his respects.

I'll say again that most musicians today are friends. But there was a time when tension between musicians was high. It was said that the great singers Bade Ghulam Ali Khansahib and Ustad Amir Khansahib were rivals. It was also generally believed that Bade Ghulam Ali Khansahib did not sing a raga in its pure form, and had a thumri and light style, while Amir Khansahib was thought of as the pure singer.

The two Khans lived in Palanpur, an area close to Opera House in Bombay. It was also home to the kothas and the baijis. Though these great singers lived in the same neighbourhood, they did not interact with each other—their students probably made the problem worse by talking up the importance of one guru over the other. Some students can create tension to prove that what they are learning is superior. But if you sat and talked with these great singers individually, which I have done, their mutual admiration was apparent.

NMK: What did your father say when he heard you had gone against his wishes and visited Kishan Maharajji's house in Benares?

ZH: Raviji never told Abba about the incident. When I returned that evening to his Shivpur home, he said: 'I know there's no problem. Kishan is a friend of mine and so is Samta Prasad, but your father asked me to look after you. You should have some regard for his wishes. I will not tell him, but you should have cleared it with me.'

NMK: It was good of him not to have mentioned it. [*pause*] Many Indian classical musicians enjoy a huge following. Is there someone whom you feel is somewhat of an unsung hero?

ZH: The sarangi master Pandit Ram Narayanji. The sarangi is one of the most difficult instruments to play because it has three main gut strings, thirty-six sympathetic strings and a resonant chamber. It's a hollow instrument. Those thirty-six sympathetic strings vibrate and resonate constantly, and if you do not hit a note precisely, you'll sound way out of tune.

The sarangi traditionally accompanied vocalists, but eventually vocalists phased it out because the tone of the sarangi is too close to the human voice and there is a constant clash. The harmonium, which is more supportive of the human voice, took over.

Pandit Ram Narayanji made great sacrifices in his own career because he wanted the sarangi to be considered as a solo instrument for the stage, so he stopped accompanying vocalists and stopped playing for films, which earned him good money. In the 1960s, he decided to give it all up so that he could establish the sarangi on a par with the sitar, sarod, surbahar and veena. So, he lost both film work and the opportunity of playing with great vocalists. But Ram Narayanji stuck to his guns and finally the sarangi did receive an elevated status. This helped sarangi players who came later, including Sultan Khansahib and Sabri Khansahib of Delhi and so on. People don't talk enough about Pandit Ram Narayanji's contribution. He was a very special musician.

Now there are about ten fine young sarangi players, including Dilshad, Sabir, Kamal Sabri and others. The sarangi has recently enjoyed a renaissance of sorts and the work that Ram Narayanji started and Sultan Khansahib followed—who could play the sarangi just as well—is being carried forward. You had Ravi Shankar–Vilayat Khan, and there was Ram Narayan–Sultan Khan.

NMK: There was another wonderful sitar player Nikhil Banerjee.

ZH: I have accompanied him many times. He was one of those musicians who had to suffer from the Ravi Shankar syndrome. Ravi Shankarji was so famous and such a great marquee name that people did not look to Vilayat Khansahib, Pandit Nikhil Banerjee or Rais Khansahib, or even to Ustad Halim Jaffer Khansahib, who passed away recently.

These sitar players did not get much attention from the media or from people in general. The media was interested in talking to Ravi Shankarji because he was a megastar. It was just the way it was. Though I did hear that Bengali audiences preferred Nikhil Banerjee to Ravi Shankarji and even to Vilayat Khansahib.

I think Nikhil Banerjee consciously tried to create a very rounded tone that had a muted projection and was not sparkly and bright. It was a very soothing tone. When you listened to Vilayat Khansahib's sitar, if the sound system was not tuned right, it could sound trebly and sharp.

Ravi Shankarji could have sounded like that too, but he added a fifth low string to his sitar, a kharaj string, which Vilayat Khansahib's sitar did not have. This meant that Ravi Shankarji could go from a very low tone to a very high tone—and the fifth string kind of compensated for the brightness. He bridged the gap between the sitar and the surbahar.

Nikhil Banerjee was an absolute genius of a musician. He was technically a very efficient sitar player and he could play fast taans and alaaps beautifully. He had that sparkle and dignified grandness. He learned music under Ustad Allauddin Khansahib, and for the most part was mentored by Ali Akbar Khansahib, whom he considered an important guide. If people wanted to hear something different, they gravitated towards Nikhil Banerjee because his musicality was of a very special kind and it had the influence of Ali Akbar Khansahib. He was a much-loved sitar player for us musicians.

NMK: And Pannalal Ghosh?

ZH: I was very young but I did hear his recordings. Pannalal Ghoshji wanted to take a folk instrument like the flute and make it acceptable as a classical musical instrument. He played a lot in films and made many songs memorable.

But the kind of boost that the film *Goonj Uthi Shehnai* gave Bismillah Khansahib and his shehnai, Panna Babu did not get, despite the popularity of the other *Goonj Uthi Shehnai* song that he had played for, '*Main piya teri tu maane ya na maane*'.

For Panna Babu to establish the flute as a classical instrument would have required many more years, but he sadly passed away in 1960, when he was only forty-nine. Then young Hariprasad Chaurasiaji came along and established a new status for the flute.

NMK: Technology has hugely impacted music globally. When did it start influencing Indian music?

ZH: The impact of technology probably started in the 1950s. The first influence in India was seen in the recording studios, where musicians of that time understood that technology would allow their music to reach audiences and how it could sound magnified tenfold.

The older generation of great maestros like Ustad Faiyaz Khansahib, Munir Khansahib, Omkarnath Thakurji and others, believed that if they were asked to sing into a microphone—at a recording or concert—it would somehow draw away their voices and they would not have any voice left. They had this particular paranoia about technology. But the later generation of musicians, including Amir Khansahib, Bade Ghulam Ali Khansahib, Begum Akhtar, Ravi Shankarji,

Dayanita Singh spent six winters between 1981 and 1986 photographing Zakir Hussain, his family and his peers for a graduation project that in 1986 became her first book. Here, Zakir Hussain is seen at his home in Simla House, Bombay.

Ustad Allarakha always encouraged his son Zakir from a young age to find his own sound and musical expression. Photograph: Dayanita Singh

At home in Simla House, Bombay. 1980s. Photograph: Dayanita Singh

Antonia Minnecola (Toni) with her
Kathak guru, Sitara Devi. Bombay. 1985.
Photographs: Dayanita Singh

Zakir Hussain on stage with his father Ustad Allarakha and Appa Jalgaonkar on harmonium. 1959 or 1960.

On his twelfth birthday. Fazal (*to Z's left*), Taufiq in family friend Khalid Almas's arms. Simla House, Bombay.

Birthday celebration with close friends and family, including Bibi Bai Almas (*to Z's right*) and his mother (*far right*).

With his family at the Taj Mahal, Agra. (*left to right*) Khurshid, Taufiq, Bavi Begum, Ustad Allarakha, Fazal and Razia. c. mid-1960s.

Playing the dhol at his sister Khurshid's nikah ceremony. Simla House. 11 January 1975.

Receiving father and son at Bombay airport following a tour in the US are (*left to right*) Khurshid, Bavi Begum, Fazal, Razia and Taufiq. December 1971.

(*left to right*) With unidentified interviewer and the great Kathak dancer, Sitara Devi, at All India Radio, New Delhi. Early 1980s.

Just before the intermission of a Hollywood Bowl concert, there was a burly hand on photographer Eric Hayes's shoulder and a thick British accent that said, 'Mr Harrison would like you to come backstage during the intermission and get some pictures of him with the Indian musicians.' That's how Eric Hayes, who was the only photographer around that evening, ended up in a dressing room with (*left to right*) Ustad Allarakha, Ustad Ali Akbar Khan, George Harrison, Pandit Ravi Shankar and Ustad Bismillah Khan. Hollywood Bowl. 4 August 1967. Photograph: Eric Hayes

With Ustad Ali Akbar Khan. Palace of Fine Arts, San Francisco. November 1999.
Photograph: Susana Millman

With Pandit Ravi Shankar. Masonic Auditorium, San Francisco. October 1995.
Photograph: Susana Millman

Zakir Hussain has performed with an amazing variety of world musicians. In jazz great Herbie Hancock's words: 'Everyone wants to play with Zakir. He is able to transcend cultures and national borders.' Photograph (*left*): Susana Millman

Abba's first barsi concert, NCPA, Bombay. 3 February 2001. Tabla players from all the tabla gharanas gathered to pay their respects to Ustad Allarakha. Photograph: Rajani Kapse

Ali Akbar Khansahib and my father, understood the benefits of technology.

When the ustads had learned the art of recording and how to use the microphone effectively, they realized that they could go back into the sound booth, hear the quality of the recording and fix it, if need be. They also saw the importance of having a sound system in a concert hall—this was important because we had graduated from baithaks to large stages. The early sound systems in concert halls were basic and did not have the kind of layering that became available to us. In the early days, the speakers just threw out volume—a crackling and sometimes a very shrill sound. But somehow the singers' voices and the instruments did not get distorted, so audiences who were sitting in the back rows could now be reached and that was very good.

When I moved to America in the early 1970s and Mickey and I formed a partnership, I started working in his studio which was called Rolling Thunder and sometimes the Barn. I was one of the team who helped to set up the recording machines. I learned how to plug in microphones and how to use the soundboard. In that process, I discovered the kind of frequencies that worked best for Indian instruments and how they could sound better by using graphic equalizers.

So, naturally, I brought that information to the engineers who were amplifying the concert halls back in India, and when that happened, it allowed me to play my instrument differently.

NMK: Can you elaborate?

ZH: By enhancing, say, 800Hz on the graphic equalizer, I was able to lengthen the resonance of the tabla. And by adding

120Hz to the bayan made the bass sound more round and deeper, gave it much more punch.

I realized that I didn't have to work so hard. I could use the frequencies and the strength of the volume available to me to enhance certain nuances of the instrument and try to create more melodic and sweeter tones. I could be subtle, and use the sound system to bring out the best possible tones with the least possible effort.

This was something that Ravi Shankarji knew very well. Later, Hariprasad Chaurasiaji, Shivkumar Sharmaji, Amjad Ali Khansahib and many others, knew how to do the same effectively.

NMK: You're saying that working with Mickey Hart allowed you to understand the sound of the tabla as projected through a microphone?

ZH: And how the amplification can bring to the audience the most natural possible sound of the instrument and make the best use of the amplifiers and speakers. By using the low end and the mids and the high end in a balanced format—how shall I put it? It can paint a multidimensional layered sound for the audience.

I didn't want the tabla to sound very electric—or something like a mutant. I wanted to somehow retain its natural tones, and at the same time, enhance them. Look at it this way—when you listen to an instrument from five feet away, it sounds a certain way, but if you listen to the instrument with your ear almost attached to it, it sounds like a whole different world. You'll hear the lows, the mids, the highs and all sorts of sounds. The resonance just comes through so beautifully and clearly when your ear is next to it. That's what the sound system should do—bring the sound of the instrument to 5,000 people and yet sound like your ear is right next to the instrument.

NMK: To enhance the presence.

ZH: Without distorting the sound of the instrument.

NMK: And how does Mujeeb Dadarkar come into the picture?

ZH: When you know what your instrument should sound like in a concert hall and you're on the stage, you're hoping that you have a sound engineer out there who understands the electronic world, the sound system, the soundboard, and who knows the environment intimately. In addition, someone who can also analyse the sound of Zakir Hussain and his tabla, Fazal Qureshi and his tabla, Anindo Chatterjee and his tabla, and who knows exactly what to do to bring out the tonal qualities specific to these different musicians.

Mujeeb has worked with musicians for years and has worked intimately with music itself. He has spent hours with Vilayat Khansahib and Bismillah Khansahib at Doordarshan, and Ali Akbar Khansahib, during his concert tours. He has done sound for other maestros, including Amjad Ali Khansahib and Shivkumar Sharmaji. Over the years, Mujeeb has understood how to correctly project the sound of Indian instruments all the way from the audience in the first row to the back row.

NMK: When did you meet Mujeeb Dadarkar?

ZH: I met him before we actually started working together. We used to meet on a regular basis when I was composing music for Rahul Bose's film *Everybody Says I'm Fine!* Mujeeb was the sound designer.

NMK: The film was released in 2001. So, you grew close around that time?

ZH: We came to know each other better around then. I would tell him how the instruments should sound through the sound system and how I had arrived at my understanding of what needed to be done to achieve the sound that I liked.

Mujeeb and I often discussed things. Sometimes he would say: 'This instrument was not made the way it should have been made. It's not projecting the way it should.' Just the other day, during the intermission of a concert, he said: 'Your bayan is not sounding the way it normally does. I am not able to coax the kind of a tone you want.' And the funny thing was that, whilst I was playing, I noticed that the bayan had thinned out a bit and was not giving me the punch I needed. So, I swapped the bayan for another one, and then everything was fine. To have an engineer who can tell you this is fantastic. As long as it's loud, most engineers just say it sounds fine. Mujeeb is more concerned about the quality of sound, and not just the volume. He is that sort of a sensitive engineer. Because he understands music and the sounds of the instruments, he believes he should help to project the right sound. I am lucky that he finds the time to help us out in this manner, and is of course a great friend and has a great sense of humour.

NMK: It sounds like he does not compromise either.

ZH: No, he doesn't, and he will tell you exactly what's needed. That's why I have him. He will talk to the Kennedy Center team and say: 'Sorry, this is the mic and soundboard I need. The stage riser has to be this high and the microphone stand needs to be this far away.'

He is also constantly on the lookout for new equipment. Just because we have arrived at a workable place, it doesn't mean that it can't get better.

NMK: At some concerts, we hear terrible feedback—that high-pitched screeching sound. Is that something that Mujeeb can correct very quickly?

ZH: Feedback is a common problem for Indian musicians. The reason why they ask the sound engineer to turn up the on-stage speaker volume is that they want to hear what the music sounds like in the hall. When the sound returns to the stage, it enters the musician's microphone, and then goes back to the speaker, creating a cycle of sound, a loop that just runs into itself. Eventually the wires, or the sound lanes, cannot take it anymore and so it becomes one loud whistle.

The reason I am telling you all this is that I was exactly like the other Indian musicians. I wanted to hear the sound as loudly as it could be heard in the hall. But over the years I've realized that's suicidal. You must trust the sound engineer to give the audience a great sound landscape, whilst setting up a small speaker on the stage. That small speaker is not going to give you a gigantic sound, but it'll give you enough to keep you in tune and in pitch and in time with your fellow musicians.

NMK: You know a lot about sound technology—that's impressive and so useful. [*pause*] I hear that you give an average of 150 concerts a year, travelling the world all the year round—there must be a huge pressure on your time. What does time mean to you now?

ZH: For someone like Bade Ghulam Ali Khansahib, time was his servant. The same was true of Ali Akbar Khansahib. There was enough time for everything.

What does time mean to me? In this day and age, hoping that time is your ally is wishful thinking. I am not going to say that I have all the time in the world to do what I want to do. But I will say that time has been an opportune friend—I think of the time I was born, when I started playing music, the company I have kept, the people I was drawn to, the musicians I've accompanied, the kind of knowledge I have received—in that sense, time has been an opportune friend.

Today I can look back and say I have played with, and hung out with, four generations of musicians. And the fifth generation is not far away. And I'm still here with some years left in me. It is amazing that my colleagues are also my peers. Amjad Ali Khansahib is only five or six years my senior, but Shivkumar Sharmaji, Hariprasadji, Jasrajji, are much older, and yet they are my colleagues. The difference is that they were in their thirties and I was eighteen when we started on a journey together.

NMK: Do you think time passes by too quickly?

ZH: Obviously there is not enough time in the day to do everything I need to do, so I do get exhausted. Like right now,

I am really tired, but we have to work on the book. So, we're talking. I didn't sleep last night. We finished the concert in Dubai at 11 p.m., went to the hotel, had dinner, packed and went to the airport at 2.30 a.m. We took the 4 a.m. flight, landed in Bombay and I had to settle all the other musicians I was travelling with into their hotels—there was a problem and the hotel would not allow Dave Holland to take his bass into his room. All sort of craziness was happening.

So, this is how life is at the moment. I do know I have chosen it to be so. I am not in a position to complain, and shouldn't. Eventually I am the one who says yes. In that sense, time is my ally and my hurdle. I am thinking of that famous Ray Cummings quote: 'Time is what prevents everything from happening at once.'

NMK: That's a great quote. Dealing with time pressures is difficult. May I ask what makes you angry?

ZH: Ten or twelve years ago, I used to get angry more than I do now. Seven out of ten things that I would like to happen do happen nowadays. So, the need to be angry has lessened and I also realize that anger accomplishes nothing. When you get older, you realize that. But once I cross seventy, I'll turn into an irritable old man. I am sure that will happen. [*smiles*]

When I started working in America as a teacher, I was teaching people about an art form that they did not grow up with. It had to be drilled into them and that required a lot of patience. Then I joined Ali Akbar Khansahib's music school, where I had about forty students and taught them individually for six days a week, from ten in the morning to nine at night.

That's when I understood that patience is something I needed to have. Even now, when I mentor, I try to explain things in great detail. In India, we did not question our teachers. But I believe I must explain what was inexplicable about thirty-five years ago. It's a responsibility I take seriously.

As a person, I have become far more patient over the years and that has happened thanks to teaching.

NMK: Was musical notation taught at your school?

ZH: We had a class in Western music at St Michael's. That was so unusual. The teacher taught us Portuguese songs because he was from Goa. I remember playing the tabla with some Christian kids who were studying music because their parents were film musicians. In fact, a group of us represented our school on a show on All India Radio. I even acted in a school play and played the tabla at school concerts.

You asked about musical notation? I can read Indian notation, and I can read some Western notation. We do not need to look at music sheets to play, and therefore the practice of reading note by note in real time as you are performing is not part of my musical upbringing. But if I look at sheet music, I can tell E-flat from C-sharp.

NMK: How did you go about writing your symphony?

ZH: We now have tools like the software Sibelius. It is named after the famous Finnish composer. You take a midi keyboard and run it through to your computer, play the notes you want and the computer will print them out. Sibelius can assign the melodic line to a particular instrument and tell you whether that instrument has the range to execute the melodic line you want. If the instrument does not have the range, it will suggest another instrument. That kind of help is available now.

I can play the piano. Two days ago, I was playing some chords at rehearsals with Sanjay Divecha and Avishai Cohen, and Sanjay asked me: 'Zakir Bhai, where did you learn all these chords?' I said: 'I just play as I hear the tune. I can logically presume that this note works with that note, and if E is equal to B, B is equal to C, therefore E is equal to C.'

If you are a computer programmer, you can be a music composer today. You don't have to know about music—that's what's happening with a lot of DJs and remix artists. Many don't have what you may call formal musical education, but they have an ear for music and are very good with computers.

For a classical khayal singer, for example, Raga Malkauns has to be sung only in a certain way. The composer A.R. Rahman can take Raga Malkauns and create a harmonic element in it, which may not be prescribed in Malkauns, but it will sound beautiful. So, that kind of sensibility is advantageous to someone like me who is writing a symphonic piece, because I am not bound by the dos and don'ts of the Western classical world.

NMK: I went to hear you play at the NCPA recently. Your camaraderie with the jazz musicians that you were performing with was electric. I am talking about your concert with Avishai Cohen, Sanjay Divecha and Abhinav Khokhar.

You also mentioned that you'll soon be doing an album with Herbie Hancock, the great jazz musician. Do you know him well?

ZH: I had the privilege of hanging out with Mr Hancock in the 1970s, when we were touring with Shakti. Many bands toured on the summer jazz circuit in Europe and so did Shakti. In those days, the band managers would pool resources and sell the concert as a package to the organizer or promoter. Your band, my band, his band, were all put together, and this meant cutting down on costs, hiring buses, travelling together and sharing hotel expenses, etc. So, Herbie Hancock's band, Shakti and Billy Cobham/George Duke's band toured together. At some point, Weather Report joined us too.

That's how I have a long association with Herbie Hancock. We toured and then we all moved on. Every now and then we'd meet and do projects together. Like three years ago, Herbie, Carlos Santana and I played together at the Hollywood Bowl in LA, and in Istanbul two years ago on International Jazz Day. Mr Hancock wants me to help him finish a record that he's doing.

NMK: Do you find that you have a different kind of relationship with a jazz musician, as opposed to an Indian musician?

ZH: For me it's kind of the same because I grew up in both worlds. Sometimes people ask, where did you grow up? I don't consider my first eighteen years in India as where I really grew up. It was a protected world from where I occasionally stepped out and travelled and performed, but mostly I was at home being looked after like a prince. I was thrown into the deep end and had to find my way when I was eighteen and had just arrived in America. That was really the point from where I broke the shackles of being a young spoilt Indian kid and tried to grow up in the world of jazz and rock and pop. I managed to get into that life seamlessly and did not suffer a culture shock. It was all quite natural. I was lucky that way.

NMK: I know you have a hectic schedule. Do you have a team that supports you?

ZH: I was pretty much on my own in the early years in America. I was not a star or a well-known person and had very few concert opportunities, so I couldn't afford an assistant or a road manager. Basically I was doing all that myself. Travelling in buses, sitting in cramped economy seats, and carrying the tabla—that's where the wear and tear has affected the body.

Ravi Shankarji was probably the first Indian musician who had a staff of some sort, and later a management agency looked after him. In India, you don't usually have managing agents, but secretaries and personal managers. A manager's protection of the artist is sometimes interpreted as a display of power. The secretaries of some Indian stars are regarded as Hitlers.

The great singer Mohammed Rafi's brother-in-law, Zaheer [Ahmad], was his secretary. Nobody liked him because he was very protective of Rafi Sahib. Many people thought it was Zaheer who did not allow Rafi Sahib to sing for less money. But looking back, one can understand that Zaheer was just looking after Rafi Sahib's best interests, and he was doing what this great singer could not do himself—saying no—and keeping at bay certain things that needed to be kept at bay. It was obvious to people that their relationship was deep because within six months of Rafi Sahib's passing, Zaheer died. He was heartbroken because they were so close.

From 1986, when I began to tour extensively with Abba, my wife Toni took over the administrative part of my life. That was a godsend. By the early years of the millennium, it became very difficult for Toni to do all that, plus run the house, the recording label and look after our girls. She was not able to concentrate on her dance. In the meantime, I had become more popular and several management companies approached me. We went to New York and had meetings with different people and finally settled on IMG to manage me. They have been running my life for the last ten or eleven years in America and Europe.

In India, I have a secretary, Nirmala Bachani. She is efficient and very protective. She's nice and very honest and she cares. It's rare to find somebody who does not prioritize her personal agenda. Sometimes I feel a little bad for Nirmala that maybe she should have expanded her horizons and managed and taken care of a roster of musicians. To her credit, she has never complained and does not seem to feel that she should expand. For almost fourteen years, she has been there to watch my back. Some people do have ambitions, and want to make a lot more money. But Nirmala is on a different shelf. I am very lucky in that way.

NMK: What about Shaukat Apa, who looks after your Simla House home? She has history written in every line of her face.

ZH: Shaukat Apa is family. Her job is to cook and make sure the house is kept clean. If she doesn't want to cook, she doesn't have to. She has been with us since she was a baby. Her mother and her grandmother were with us from the Mahim days. Shaukat Apa's sister lived with us too and then she moved to UAE to work. As long as my mother was there, Shaukat Apa was provided for, and after my mother passed away, I decided that Shaukat Apa should have a salary because I am not always around to look after her.

So, Nirmala oversees my business affairs in India, and Shaukat Apa runs the house in the way she wants. I don't have a driver, but I have a car service that I use and they have assigned a driver to me who is always with me. There's also Rocky, who cleans the flat under Shaukat Apa's watchful eye. He has a lively personality. He's very nice and very responsible. Rocky recently needed some money for his sister's wedding and I gave it to him and he has paid it all back. You look at this kid and you can see he has integrity.

NMK: I am wondering what makes you happy, other than your granddaughter?

ZH: Well, let's see. Being with my family makes me happy. A good concert makes me happy, when my fellow musicians and I create an interesting musical moment. Watching a beautiful game of tennis makes me happy.

NMK: And when you're performing, are you someone else?

ZH: No, it's the real me. It's like being at home with your wife and you are utterly yourself. I have a similar relationship with the spirit of music—I don't feel the need to hide behind anything. When I sit and talk about social things, I may give off a whole different persona, but as a tabla player, I am who I am.

We are fortunate that we musicians can be ourselves. It's a glorious moment when we are able to open up in front of the audience. At the same time, you also have to be crazy to want that spot. You must have a large ego.

NMK: A large ego? Why?

ZH: Oh, absolutely—who am I kidding? I love the attention. I love the adulation. It's a great feeling, and as a child I loved it too. When I was playing, it was like—oh, everybody is looking at me and clapping. I am the centre of attention.

NMK: You believed the adulation?

ZH: Oh yeah, I'm sure I did, till I was sixteen. At sixteen I got a really bad review—the music critic and musicologist of *The Times of India*, Mr Mohan Nadkarni, essentially said that I had all the technique, but had not grown as an artist. Yeah, it was harsh. I had already been playing professionally for four years, and so the critic was looking for some forward movement, and not for the same old package. At first it destroyed me and I got very upset and very sad, and then it made sense. It totally did.

I had to find a way of reinventing myself, rediscovering myself. It was important for me to prove that critic wrong. Some years later I actually thanked Mr Nadkarni for making me rethink things because that's when I decided to go for a chilla.

NMK: Can you tell me about the 'chilla'?

ZH: It's also called 'chilla katna'. It is associated with Sufis and musicians. A chilla is a kind of a spiritual retreat.

Some people take a vow of silence for days, and others go to a remote place to be alone with their music or meditation. They say if you do three chillas in a lifetime, it completes the rituals of becoming a man of music, not just a boy of music—like a native American climbing a mountain and plucking an eagle's feather or something.

NMK: A kind of rite of passage?

ZH: Yes, a kind of rite of passage. During the chilla, you're alone and have to fend for yourself, eat certain foods and have no contact with the outside world—concentrate totally on what you do. If you're a tabla player, you play tabla. If you're a singer, you sing, etc.

Music in its basic sense is vibrations. So, if you play for fifteen to sixteen hours in a day, you sense a whole lot of vibrations that have an effect on you. You can get into a trance and in that state of mind you end up revisiting experiences that you have perhaps buried. If you have been through a rough time in your life, dark thoughts resurface. So you come out of the chilla either feeling totally broken or totally enlightened; it depends on your state of mind.

When I decided to do my first chilla, I was about sixteen. Normally I would have asked Abba for his permission, but I couldn't, because he was somewhere in England, touring with Ravi Shankarji. I headed off to the shrine of a Muslim saint called Haji Malang. The shrine is a three-hour climb from Malangadd Fort, near Kalyan. It was not the first time I had been there. As a child, my mother had taken me there because I was always ill. She took a mannat at the shrine that if I got well again, she would distribute sweetmeats, equivalent to my body weight, to the poor. I know that she kept her promise.

The maximum time of a chilla is forty days: that's really Biblical, isn't it? But I only stayed sixteen days at the shrine. During that time, I recited rhythms, which could sound like chanting, and played tabla for hours and hours every day. And then one day I had a visitation. I really did. When I returned home, far from being downhearted, I felt elated.

Some weeks later, Abba returned home. My mother told him that I had just taken off. He was absolutely furious. What if something had gone wrong during the chilla? When Abba calmed down, he asked me what I did there. I explained that I had spent hours practising and added: 'You know I had this visitation. An elderly gentleman came and recited a rhythmic composition to me.' I told Abba the composition was very clear in my mind and I played it for him.

He went very quiet and then started pacing up and down. Abba had this habit of putting his hands behind his back when he walked. After a little while, he said: 'Play it again.' I did. I don't know what was disturbing Abba, but I could tell that he was struggling to understand what I had experienced.

Later that night, he said: 'This is a very old composition. I have not taught it to you, and I know that you didn't know it before. Most of my students don't know it either. Describe the man to me.' I described the person I saw as best I could—a white-haired dignified-looking man wearing a pagdi, a long kameez and salwar. Abba said: 'This composition is by Baba Malang, and your description fits the saint's description. Maybe you had a visitation from him.'

These things are inexplicable, and I don't like to talk about it because I am never really sure.

NMK: But it did happen?

ZH: It did happen. Every year on Guru Purnima, the day you honour your guru, I fly in from California. All Abba's students get together, and we have a little gathering to honour our teacher. Everyone plays something. There have been times around Guru Purnima that I have gone to sleep and the next day when I wake up, I find that a new rhythmic idea has popped up in my head. If belief has a place in your life, you accept, if not, you take it as the inexplicable.

NMK: What prompted you to do a second chilla?

ZH: I was in Seattle, studying and working at the University of Washington. I was hanging out in the ethnomusicology department with my colleagues. There was Mr Abraham, the African music teacher, the Indonesian gamelan ensemble and some other friends who attended the jazz class.

But then, you know how it is—a stage comes in your life where you are creatively empty, the box has nothing left. It happens and it's a frightening place to be in. Sometimes the workload keeps you so occupied with the responsibility to be creative on stage every night that you do not realize that your mind has gone blank. Suddenly, you can't think of anything fresh to present and, as a defence mechanism, you go on autopilot. This is not uncommon; it just means that you did not have the time to step back and recharge, to clear your mind from the thousand or so combinations and permutations that you have used so far. In short, you have run out of GB space and need to wipe the mind's hard drive so that you can load up new software to write new programmes!

That's why I decided to do a second chilla. I did not see any friends during those days. I taught at the university for about two-and-half hours and then spent the rest of the day alone in my small apartment. I had to cut off from everything to find my way again.

I also realized that you could be anywhere, if you wanted to connect to your inner self. I was in Seattle and not in a hut in Punjab or at the Haji Malang shrine. But I was convinced that if my focus was sincere and genuine, the spirits would help me to find my way out of the quagmire.

I believe that this second chilla gave me new insight into how I could expand my instrument's reach. It made me realize that adulation and applause are not the centre of creativity. Being true to yourself and to your abilities, standing behind your efforts without the fear of criticism should be the goal. This unshackling of the mind prepared me for my impending association with Ali Akbar Khansahib, Mickey Hart, John McLaughlin and other greats.

NMK: Would you attempt a third chilla?

ZH: I don't feel the need to do a third chilla. Somehow I believe that all the years of working, interacting, learning, travelling all around the world, have been like a chilla. I think there is something very mysterious about doing a chilla, but half the time, people do it because they want to get away from everything.

NMK: Do you meditate?

ZH: What do you call meditation? Centring your focus? Making sure that your body aligns itself so that the core has been strengthened. Ironing my kurta is meditation for me. Every crease is very clearly seen to, every little *shal* in the pyjama is being watched; it's not vanity. It's just concentration. Some people have beads, others have a meditation bowl in which they rotate a stick and it vibrates and creates a tone and they focus on that. I have my kurta and the iron.

Getting ready for a concert, focusing on it, selecting the instrument that I need for the evening and tuning it—that whole process is meditation for me. It's not sitting cross-legged in a lotus position, closing your eyes and taking deep breaths. Emptying your mind is the first law of meditation. Just throwing everything out and then reorganizing. For me, emptying my mind is not the issue. It is organizing my mind in an orderly fashion, so that when I speak my music, it comes out as Chapter 1, 2, 3, etc., and not Chapter 1, 5, 7. It should not be muddled.

I have come to terms with the fact that I am fallible, I am human, and at the same time I am not doing something fantastic and incredible, it's just normal. I remind myself that I am no different from a surgeon or doctor, engineer or cook. They're all good at what they do. It does not mean that I stand on a higher pedestal, just because I am an artist.

NMK: Will you not miss the adulation if it goes away?

ZH: I don't think I'll miss it. I am very happy where I am, and that really has nothing to do with adulation. I am happy that at this age I am in this place. I started very early in life.

I realize I am good at certain things and not at others. I'm definitely a bad actor, so there's no reason to ever attempt acting again. I know I am a good tabla player, so I want to continue playing. I can do music well, so I can compose. But for me to think that I could sing is not a good idea.

I know there is no point in dwelling on the past because that's done, it's gone, and it's over. So tomorrow I hope to create something different. I don't want to fool my audience. I want to give them something that will satisfy me. It doesn't matter how bad it is, or how good. That's irrelevant. I love what I do. I love my relationship with my instrument. So, when I'm on the stage, I am not afraid to share that happiness. I think I've arrived at the same point where my father was, vis-à-vis his instrument and his music.

Success is not how many Grammys you win or how many platinum records you have. Success is standing tall behind something and saying—this is what I wanted. I am one of those musicians who came at the cusp of a great change in the music world and I was carried on that wave. I had the good fortune to establish a very unhurried relationship with music, and at the same time, the wave took me places. Otherwise, I would have to run to keep up. I was already sitting on the bus before it drove off.

Index

'Aadmi ko chhahiye waqt se darr kar rahe', 38
Aandhiyan, 27, 28
'Aap ki nazron ne samjha...', 21, 98–99
Abraham, Mr, 175
Ahmad, Zaheer, 169
Akhtar, Begum, 113–14, 91, 158
Akhtar, Javed, 20, 21, 22
Ali Akbar College of Music, 65, 119
Ali, Naushad, 26, 33
'Allah tero naam', 28
Alla Rakha Foundation, 55
Allarakha (documentary film title), 50
Almas, Bibi Bai, 30-31, 92
Amonkar, Kishori, 88
Anand, Chetan, 27, 28
Anand, Dev, 28, 40
Anisa. *See* Phillips
Anmol Ghadi, 70
Annapurna Devi, 68, 137
Ashok Kumar, 1, 40

Asif, K., 25–26, 40
Asimov, Isaac, 17
Aulia, Khurshid (sister), 3, 20, 29, 54–55, 79
Aulia, Ayub (brother-in-law), 55
Aulia, Ghazal (niece), 55
Aulia, Ameer Najeeb (nephew), 55
Aulia, Mukarram Zaki (nephew), 55
'Awaaz de kahaan hai', 70
Azmi, Kaifi, 20, 39
Azmi, Shabana, 39, 118

Bachani, Nirmala, 145, 170–71
Baksh, Qadir, Mian, 23, 47–48, 49, 105, 139
Banerjee, Nikhil, Pandit, 137, 156–57
Banks, Louiz, 80
Bertolucci, Bernardo, 125–28
Bhatkhande, V.N., 134–35
Bhosle, Asha, 42, 131
Bilquis (sister), 54, 56

Index

Birdman, 122
Bose, Rahul, 130, 162
Burman, R.D., 38, 124
Burman, S.D., 28, 34
Butler, Michael, 75

Chatterjee, Anindo, Pandit, 136, 161
Chaudhuri, Swapan, Pandit, 136
Chaurasia, Hariprasad, Pandit, 25, 36, 58, 79, 111, 129, 137, 158, 160, 164
Chaurasia, Rakesh, 9, 127, 130, 144, 145, 146
Cobham, Billy, 168
Cohen, Avishai, 167

Dadarkar, Mujeeb, 161–63
Davis, Miles, 17, 135
Diga Rhythm Band, 105
Divecha, Sanjay, 167
Duke, George, 168
Dutt, Nargis, 1, 37

Elfman, Danny, 124
Eliot, T.S., 18
Everybody Says I'm Fine!, 162

Faiz Ahmad Faiz, 18
Famous Studio, 34, 35
Federer, Roger, 18
Fleck, Béla, 78, 96
Flye, Tom, 106

Ganga Bai, 89
Gauhar Jaan, 91, 149
Ghosal, Sumantra, ix, 115, 130
Ghosh, Pannalal, Pandit, 157–58
Girija Devi, 90
Global Drum Project, The, 107
Goonj Uthi Shehnai, 116, 158
Grateful Dead, 108, 131
Gulzar, 21, 22
Gurtu, Shobha, 88
Gyani Baba, 2–3, 54

Haji Malang, 173–74, 176
Hancock, Herbie, 82, 84, 167–68
Harland, Eric, 82, 130
Hart, Mickey, 82, 100, 102, 105–6, 111, 129, 159, 160, 176
Drumming at the Edge of Magic: A Journey into the Spirit of Percussion, 49, 105–6
Hassan, Mehdi, 70
Hazrat Imam Hussain, 2, 4
Heat and Dust, 114, 121
Herrmann, Bernard, 124
Householder, The, 27
Hum Dono, 27, 28
Hungry Stones, 27
Husain, M.F., 123
Hussain, Faizan (nephew), 144
Hussain, Sajjad, 27, 40–41, 42, 43

Index

IMG Artists Ltd., 78, 170
Inquilab, 22, 55
Iqbal, 34
Ivory, James, 121

'*Jab pyaar kiya toh darna kya*', 25
Jaidev, 27–28, 41
Jarre, Maurice, 124
Jasraj, Pandit, 88, 113, 164
Jaws, 124–25
Joshi, Bhimsen, Pandit, 88

'*Ka karun sajni aaye na balaam*', 94
Kapoor, Jennifer Kendal, 14
Kapoor, Prithviraj, 24
Kapoor, Raj, 1, 40
Karuna Supreme, 108
Katrak, Minoo, 35
Keer, Maruti, 34
Khan, Aashish, 71, 76
Khan, Ali Akbar, Ustad, 17, 27, 28, 63–76, 77, 91, 94, 98–100, 103, 108, 111, 119, 138, 157, 158–59, 161, 164, 165, 176
Khan, Allauddin, Ustad, 65–66, 137, 157
Khan, Amaan Ali, Ustad, 40
Khan, Amir, Ustad, 17, 91, 154, 158
Khan, Amir Hussain, Ustad, 103
Khan, Amjad Ali, Ustad, 58, 60, 160, 161, 164
Khan, Ashiq Ali, Ustad, 48, 89

Khan, Bade Ghulam Ali, Ustad, 4, 17, 26, 48, 88, 89, 94, 154, 158, 164
Khan, Bismillah, Ustad, 13, 99, 113, 114–16, 151, 158, 161
Khan, Dilshad, 9, 156
Khan, Faiyaz, Ustad, 91, 158
Khan, Ghulam Mustafa, Ustad, 88
Khan, Habibuddin, Ustad, 103
Khan, Halim Jaffer, Ustad, 152, 156
Khan, Mehboob, 70
Khan, Munawar Ali, Ustad, 88
Khan, Nisar Hussain, Ustad, 90
Khan, Rais, Ustad, 25, 156
Khan, Raja Mehdi Ali, 21
Khan, Sabir, 9, 156
Khan, Sabri, Ustad, 156
Khan, Sultan, Ustad, 56, 57, 99–100, 115, 140, 156
Khan, Shafaat Ahmed, Ustad, 151
Khan, Vilayat, Ustad, 13, 87, 91–92, 94, 97–99, 103, 113, 115, 136, 151, 156, 157, 161
Khayyam, 41
Khokhar, Abhinav, 167
Khurshid Apa. *See* Aulia, Khurshid
Kumar, Dilip, 26, 40, 122
Kumar Gandharva, Pandit, 136
Kumar, Kishore, 24
Kumar, Niladri, 9, 130, 144

Lala Bhai, 34
Last Emperor, The, 126

Laxmikant-Pyarelal, 38, 124
Lieberman, Fredric, 105
Little Buddha, 125–28
Lloyd, Charles, 78, 82–83, 130
London Philharmonic Orchestra, 126
Ludhianvi, Sahir, 28, 38
Lynn McDowell, Judy, 75-76

Maa Baap, 24
Madari, 24
Madhubala, 37
Mahadevan, Shankar, 38, 80
Maharaj, Birju, Pandit, 31, 92–93, 152
Maharaj, Chaube, Pandit, 92-93
Maharaj, Kanthe, Pandit, 103, 136
Maharaj, Kishan, Pandit, viii, 23, 95, 103, 136, 151, 153-55
'*Main piya teri tu maane ya na maane*', 158
'*Main zindagi ka saath nibhaata chala gaya*', 28
Maharaj, Pooran, Pandit, 153
Makeba, Miriam, 146
Malang, Haji, 173, 176
Mangeshkar, Lata, 21, 24, 27, 37, 40, 41, 42
McLaughlin, John, 85, 102, 108, 111, 129, 130, 176
Mehboob Recording Studio, 34, 43
Menuhin, Yehudi, 64
Merchant–Ivory, 27, 125

Minnecola, Antonia, (Toni, wife), 18, 53, 55, 75–80, 117, 119, 120, 169
Mohan, Madan, 21, 28, 33, 34, 45, 132
Mohan Studio, 25–26, 29, 34
Moment Records, 78
'*Mora nadaan balma na jaane dil ki baat*', 37
Moreira, Airto, 106
Mughal-e-Azam, 25
Mukesh, 24
Mukherjee, Budhaditya, Pandit, 138
Munawar (brother), 54, 55
Moradabadi, Jigar, 21

Nadkarni, Mohan, 172
'*Nahin aaye sawariya ghir aaye badariya*', 90
Narayan, Ram, Pandit, 25, 155–56
Navketan Films, 28
Nayyar, O.P., 20
Nigam, Sonu, 42, 94
Nigar, Sultana, 25
Nirmala Devi, 88
Noor Jehan, 70, 74

'*O jaanewaale ruk ja koi dam*', 27
Olatunji, Babatunde, 106

Pajama Game, The, 119
Paranjpye, Sai, 121
Parker, Charlie Bird, 17

Index

Peraza, Armando, 85–87
Phillips, Anisa (daughter), 53, 79, 81, 118–19
Phillips, Taylor (son-in-law), 118
Phillips, Zara (granddaughter), 119
Planet Drum, 105, 106–7
Prasad, Laxman, Jaipurwale, 133
Prasad, Samta, Pandit, viii, 92, 103, 136, 151, 154–55
Prithvi Theatre, 13, 14
Pyarelal. *See* Laxmikant-Pyarelal

Qureshi, Allarakha, Ustad, (Abba), viii, 1, 2, 3, 4, 5–6, 8, 10, 16, 17, 22, 23–26, 29, 30, 31–32, 38, 39–40, 41, 42, 45, 46–51, 55, 57–61, 67, 73, 76, 78, 87, 88–89, 94, 101–2, 103, 112–13, 116–17, 132, 133, 138, 142–43, 151, 152–53, 155, 159, 169, 173, 174
Qureshi, Bavi Begum Allarakha (Amma), 2, 29–30, 31, 33, 39, 46, 50, 51–52, 58, 61, 76, 78, 79, 101–2, 112, 117, 173–74
Qureshi, Birwa (sister-in-law), 53, 144
Qureshi, Fazal (brother), 24, 53, 54, 56, 57, 58, 142, 144, 161
   Alia (Fazal and Birwa's daughter), 144
   Azann (Fazal and Birwa's son), 144
Qureshi, Geetika Varde (sister-in-law), 53, 143–44
   Shikharnaad (Taufiq and Geetika's son), 144
Qureshi, Hashim Ali (grandfather), 46
Qureshi, Isabella (daughter), 53, 79, 119
Qureshi, Taufiq (brother), 24, 53, 54, 57, 58, 143
Qureshi, Zakir Hussain
   birth, 1
   childhood, 2–5
   education, 30–32, 34, 45–46, 52, 61, 117
   marriage, 76–77
   naming, 2

'Raat bhi hai kuchh bheegi bheegi', 28
Rafi, Mohammed, 24, 169
Raga, a journey to the soul of India, 65
Rahman, A.R., 38, 39, 167
Rahman, Habiba, 30–31
Ray, Satyajit, 27
Razia Apa (sister), 29, 54, 56–57, 58, 59, 60, 144
   Afshan (Razia's daughter), 144
   Faizan (Razia's son), 144
Reshma aur Shera, 28

Index

Rhythm Devils, 105
Rich, Buddy, 102
'Rind jo mujhko samajhte hain unhen hosh nahin', 21
Roshan, 20, 28, 33
Roy, Bimal, 25, 27, 40

Saaz, 121
Sakamoto, Ryuichi, 126–27
Salim-Suleiman, 38
Samanta, Shakti, 25
Santana, Carlos, 85, 168
Sayani, Ayesha, ix, 115
Shaikh, Afshan Hussain (niece) 144
Shakti, viii, 85, 107–8, 167–68
Shankar, L., 85, 108, 110
Shankar, Lakshmi, 51–52
Shankar–Ehsaan–Loy, 38
Shankar, Ravi, Pandit, 8, 11, 17, 18, 29, 58, 64–67, 69, 77, 87, 94, 97, 98, 103, 111, 113, 136, 138, 149, 151–53, 156–58, 160, 169, 173
  My Music, My Life, 18
Shankar, Rajendra, 51
Sharma, Rahul, 144
Sharma, Shivkumar, Pandit, 25, 58, 79, 111, 113, 129, 130, 160, 161, 164
Shaukat Apa, 19, 170–71
Sinha, Tapan, 27

Sitara Devi, 25, 31, 78, 92–93, 111
Sood, Daman, 35
Soweto Choir, 146, 148
Speaking Hand, The: Zakir Hussain and the Art of the Indian Drum, ix
Star Wars, 120, 124
Sultanpuri, Majrooh, 18, 20, 37
'Suno chhoti si gudiya ki lambi kahaani', 27
Sur Singar Samsad, 92

'Tere pyaar mein ruswa ho kar jaayen kahaan deewane log', 70
Thakur, Omkarnath, Pandit, 88, 158
Thirakwa, Ahmedjaan, Ustad, 23, 103, 136
Toni. *See* Minnecola, Antonia
Tripathi, Abu, 153
Tripathi, Anju, 153
Tripathi, Kamalapati, 153

Ustad Allarakha Institute of Music, Mumbai, 142

Vhatkar, Haridas, 96–97
Vinayakram, T.H. (Vikkuji), 20, 85, 106, 108–9

Wavy Gravy, 131
Williams, John, 124–25
Winehouse, Amy, 131

Acknowledgements

My deepest gratitude goes to Antonia Minnecola (Toni), who has helped at every stage of this book. Her meticulous eye for detail and most valuable advice are much appreciated. I am most grateful for the assistance of Nirmala Bachani, Khurshid Aulia, the Alla Rakha Foundation, London, Ayesha Sayani, Sumantra Ghosal, Shonali Gajwani, Peter Chappell, Anisa Phillips, Isabella Qureshi, Kunal Kapoor, Shameem Kabir, Priya Kumar, Jon Page, Eric Hayes, Shahrukh Hussain, Naresh Fernandes, Urvashi Bachani, HarperCollins *Publishers* India and Shantanu Ray Chaudhuri. Special thanks to Dayanita Singh, Michael Weintrob, Susana Millman and Rakesh Chaurasia for their kind and generous permission to allow their photographs to be reproduced in this book.

About Nasreen Munni Kabir

Born in India, Nasreen Munni Kabir has written sixteen books on Hindi cinema and made several TV series on the subject for Channel 4, UK. She continues to work as their Indian cinema consultant, selecting their annual Indian film season. A former governor on the board of the British Film Institute, Nasreen lives in London.

HarperCollins *Publishers* India

At HarperCollins India, we believe in telling the best stories and finding the widest readership for our books in every format possible. We started publishing in 1992; a great deal has changed since then, but what has remained constant is the passion with which our authors write their books, the love with which readers receive them, and the sheer joy and excitement that we as publishers feel in being a part of the publishing process.

Over the years, we've had the pleasure of publishing some of the finest writing from the subcontinent and around the world, including several award-winning titles and some of the biggest bestsellers in India's publishing history. But nothing has meant more to us than the fact that millions of people have read the books we published, and that somewhere, a book of ours might have made a difference.

As we look to the future, we go back to that one word—a word which has been a driving force for us all these years.

Read.

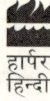